MOSCOW
POCKET GUIDE

D1555816

Walking Eye
mobile app

Discover the world's best destinations with the Insight Guides Walking Eye app, available to download for free in the App Store and Google Play.

The container app provides easy access to fantastic free content on events and activities taking place in your current location or chosen destination, with the possibility of booking, as well as the regularly-updated Insight Guides travel blog: Inspire Me. In addition, you can purchase curated, premium destination guides through the app, which feature local highlights, hotel, bar, restaurant and shopping listings, an A to Z of practical information and more. Or purchase and download Insight Guides eBooks straight to your device.

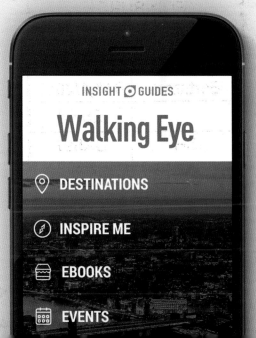

TOP 10 ATTRACTIONS

THE CHAMBERS IN ZARYADE
This atmospheric boyar home was the birthplace of the Romanov dynasty. See page 39.

BOLSHOY THEATRE
This grand theatre is the home of Russian opera and ballet. See page 44.

PUSHKIN MUSEUM
One of the world's great classical and modern art museums. See page 53.

ST BASIL'S CATHEDRAL IN RED SQUARE
Moscow's most celebrated domes. See page 37.

VICTORY PARK
This green space is a firm favourite with Russian families. See page 65.

KREMLIN
The world-famous riverside fortress is a feast of fabulous churches and princely palaces. See page 28.

MAXIM GORKY MUSEUM
The height of Moscow's *style moderne*. See page 62.

OLD AND NEW TRETYAKOV GALLERIES
The finest collection of Russian art. See pages 75 and 77.

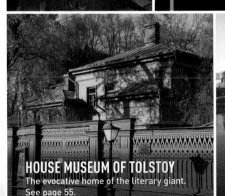

HOUSE MUSEUM OF TOLSTOY
The evocative home of the literary giant. See page 55.

NEW MAIDEN CONVENT
A jewel of Orthodox Christianity, steeped in history. See page 57.

A PERFECT DAY

9.00am

Breakfast

Start off the day with a hearty Russian breakfast at your hotel or head over to the atmospheric Bosco Bar at GUM overlooking Red Square.

1.30pm

Market treats

End your metro tour at the Tsvetnoy bulvar station. Wander around the upscale farmer's market on the fifth floor of the Tsvetnoy shopping centre (Tsvetnoy bulvar 15, str.1), sampling homemade cheeses, honey, sausages, smoked fish and other delicacies. Pick up some treats for a park-bench picnic in the boulevard park across from the market, or stop in one of the cafés on the sixth or seventh floor for a light lunch.

10.00am

Kitay-gorod

Spend the morning wending your way along the narrow lanes of medieval Moscow, where jewel-box churches and ancient mansions are tucked between *style moderne* apartment buildings and contemporary offices.

12 noon

Ride the metro

Zip down the escalator at the Ploshchad Revolutsii metro station, which has some of the best – and kitschest – sculptures of armed workers and peasants. Take the purple line to Kurskaya, and observe some of the most beautiful stations in the Moscow underground.

3.30pm

Bath time

Steam city grit and tension away in a relaxing session at the Sandunovsky Baths. Alternate steam and cold water dips until your skin becomes soft and invigorated, and then enjoy some refreshing tea (or beer) to prepare for re-entry into city life.

Classic culture

7.00pm

Spend the evening celebrating Russian culture with ballet at the Bolshoy, opera at the New Opera, or the philharmonic at the Conservatory. Stave off hunger with a caviar sandwich and glass of champagne at the buffet during intermission.

Nightcap

12.30am

End your evening with one last drink at the O-2 Lounge, on the top floor of the Ritz-Carlton. It's astronomically expensive, but the view of Red Square and the Kremlin at night are worth it.

Pick-me-up

6.00pm

Join the after-work crowd for a quick drink and snack in one of the cafés or bars on the pedestrianised Kamergersky pereulok, the Hermitage Garden, or indulge in some people-watching in Aleksandrovsky Gardens.

Chill-out time

10.30pm

Head over to Bolotny Island for a late-night snack with the bohemian and golden set at one of a dozen clubs. You might relax at the Icon Club (Bolotnaya nab. 9, str. 1). At the trendy, post-industrial Art Academy (Bersenevskaya nab. 6, str. 3) you can soak in art, films and music with your meal.

CONTENTS

INTRODUCTION

Moscow is a booming European capital with shopping malls, neon lights, pre-Revolutionary buildings, bars, traffic jams, nightclubs, and a hip young population. It has an eclectic mix of architecture. Pastel classical mansions sit next to art nouveau masterpieces, down the street from angular constructivist blocks, Soviet housing estates and state-of-the-art glass office developments. Here a visitor can find some of the world's most magnificent art and beautifully restored churches, whose golden cupolas soar above the skyline, while in the streets teenagers glide by on roller blades chatting on mobile phones, and business people lunch in sushi bars.

The seat of government and the centre of Russian arts, Moscow has some of the world's finest ballet, classical music and theatre, as well as a lively club scene. Its main sites – the Kremlin and Red Square, and the brightly coloured domes of St Basil's Cathedral – need little introduction, and nor do many of the people associated with the city. Tolstoy, Gorky and Mayakovsky are among many historical figures whose homes you can visit.

Family names

Russian people's last names are modified according to gender, so Ivan Ivanov's sister would be Olga Ivanova. Then everyone has a patronymic: a middle name that means 'son of ...' or 'daughter of...'. The male form ends in '-ich' and the female form ends in '-ovna'. So if our Ivanov siblings are the children of Mikhail, the boy would have a patronymic of Mikhailovich and the girl Mikhailovna.

A MULTINATIONAL METROPOLIS

The 10 million-plus inhabitants are multinational, with large populations from the former Soviet republics in Central Asia and the Caucasus. Although there are considerable expat communities (Chinese, Indians, Europeans, Koreans and

St Basil's Cathedral

construction workers from the Caucasus, Central Asia and Turkey), Soviet central planning left Moscow without distinct ethnic neighbourhoods. But as you sit in one of the outdoor cafés or by the window of one of the city's many coffee shops, you'll see a parade of nationalities and styles: chic young women miraculously negotiating the icy cobblestones in spike-heeled boots, old women in kerchiefs, teens with blue hair and tattoos, businessmen in European suits, priests in black cassocks, Tatar women in head scarves, and, especially during the summer months, flocks of foreign tourists.

Main streets are filled with shops and cafés, but side streets are often quiet, without a shop in sight. Service is patchy: it is generally excellent but it can also be indifferent or gruff. Persevere, and you will find warm hearts beating beneath. Life here has not been easy. Despite the relative prosperity of the 21st century, weak public institutions, corruption, and the enormous pains of transformation have taken a toll on the population. For many, including young people born after the fall of the USSR,

A busy street in Central Moscow

the communist past holds a nostalgic allure.

But that communist past is hard to find in the bustling modern city. Be prepared for the traffic: municipal authorities have not managed to deal with the enormous increase in private car ownership, so pavements double as car parks and you may get stuck in one of the city's famous traffic jams – a good reason to travel by metro.

REBUILDING THE CITY

The city is still a work in progress. Much of its transformation was effected under Mayor Yuri Luzhkov, who served from 1992 to 2010, when complaints about cronyism and corruption became too hard to ignore. The new mayor, Sergei Sobyanin, has promised to take greater account of citizens' needs as the city develops. There are sometimes complaints that things are moving too fast, that each morning Muscovites awake to new building sites where the day before there had been houses, that new underground malls and car parks are leaving buildings in danger of collapsing, and that corruption is never far away. But much of the renewal has been necessary. Most impressive has been the complete rebuilding of such historic landmarks as the Resurrection Gate on Red Square and the Kazan and Christ the Redeemer cathedrals, all torn down by Stalin who drove large boulevards through the city. The vacuum left by the collapse of communist ideology has in some part been replaced by new-found religious devotion, and congregations are large. St Basil's Cathedral was on Stalin's hit-list, too, but miraculously escaped.

His own great legacy are the magnificent 'Seven Sisters' (1947–55) skyscrapers that dot the skyline (see page 48), one of which was built for the city's university. Under Mayor Luzhkov, Zurab Tsereteli, President of the Russian Academy of Arts, became the city's unofficial 'court' architect (see page 65). His contribution includes the Victory Park memorials and the huge statue of Peter the Great on the Moscow River, a landmark that has not met with universal acclaim.

THE LANGUAGE

Street signs are in Cyrillic and Latin letters, but museums are not always well-marked, and the smaller (sometimes most interesting) sites do not have all their exhibition notes in English. An ability to read Cyrillic letters helps (see page 125).

The modern Russian language owes its written codification to two 9th-century Christian missionaries from Greece, Cyril and Methodius, who wanted to translate the Bible into the language of the Slavic people. They used Greek as the basis

THE MAGNIFICENT METRO

Few cities in the world can boast a metro system that is fast, efficient, reliable – and an essential tourist sight. Begun in 1931 to showcase the first Soviet Five-Year Plan, Moscow's metro used state-of-the-art technology to celebrate the proletariat. There are 200 stations and the wait between trains is about two minutes. At the bottom of the fast-moving escalators are magnificent halls of marble and stone, with glimmering chandeliers, mosaics, statues and bas reliefs. Each one is decorated in a different way. Many celebrate Soviet history with hardy workers, happy peasants and stalwart revolutionaries. For the best tour, take the circle line and hop out at every station – it will only cost the price of a single ticket.

for the alphabet and added another dozen letters to represent additional sounds. This language, Old Church Slavonic, is still, in modified form, used in the church.

Today English exerts a strong – and in the opinion of many Russians – pernicious influence on everyday language. As a result, the modern Russian language is now filled with words familiar to Westerners, from спорт (sport) to бар (bar) and бизнес-ланч (business lunch).

THE CLIMATE

Moscow is around the same latitude as Edinburgh. Winters are long, often overcast, snowy and cold, and the whole city seems to move underground – to the malls and metros that offer congeniality and warmth. The short, glorious summer is usually hot and sunny, and the city's abundant parks, squares and boulevards are filled with leafy trees and flowers. 'Golden autumn' is a good time for travellers who love the arts: the season begins in September when troupes return from summer touring. Only early spring (March and April) doesn't show the city at its best – although the spring festival of Maslenitsa (Butter Week) before Lent makes up in merriment for the bare branches, mud and slush.

OPEN 24 HOURS

Moscow has little sleep, especially in summer. An astonishing number of shops and services stay open 24 hours a day. There is always the buzz of traffic and the bustle of business, a theatre performance ending or a nightclub just warming up, and people keeping in touch in internet cafés through until dawn. Somewhere there is always music on the air, be it a guitar at a family party, jazz in a smoky club, or Conservatory-trained musicians playing Vivaldi in an underpass. Moscow is certainly different and it is always vibrantly alive.

A BRIEF HISTORY

The history of Moscow has always been tumultuous: attacked from east and west, burnt to the ground countless times, rocked by revolutions, altered beyond recognition according to the vision and whims of its rulers – and yet filled with magnificent works of architecture and art that have miraculously withstood the ravages of time and the trials of political and social change. The fertile area filled with rivers, lakes, fields and forests that is now Moscow had been inhabited since at least the 5th century BC by a number of Slavic and European tribes. By the 10th and 11th centuries, when princes in Kiev (now the capital of Ukraine) ruled most of today's European Russia, Moscow had become a small trading post.

The first picture of Moscow, on a 12th-century manuscript

WALLED SETTLEMENT

The town was first mentioned in the chronicles in 1147, when Prince Dolgoruky ('Long Arms') of Suzdal wrote to his ally Prince Svyatoslav in Chernigov the oft-quoted phrase: 'Come to me, brother, in Moscow...' The chronicles do not tell us much about that first meeting, but we do know that Prince Yuri Dolgoruky left his own principality for this small settlement. He surrounded it with wooden walls, and it would eventually grow to be the Moscow Kremlin.

During the first centuries of its existence, Muscovy was one principality – a kind of city-state – among many. Ruled by grand princes, these principalities sometimes fought together against common enemies, and sometimes fought each other for land and power. In 1237, Muscovy and all the principalities were conquered by Tatar-Mongols, fierce horsemen from the east. At the height of its power the Mongol Empire stretched from Poland to the Pacific Ocean and from the Arctic to the Persian Gulf, the largest land-based empire the world has ever seen. Divided into four khanates, its western territory fell under the Golden Horde and Tatar-Mongol rule lasted nearly 250 years.

THE THIRD ROME AND THE 'GATHERING OF THE RUS'

The Tatar-Mongol yoke left Moscow with a mixed legacy. While the Golden Horde exacted tributes, appointed princes, and continued their raids, they also introduced many administrative and financial institutions, and let the Orthodox Church thrive. After the 5th-century sack of Rome, the Christian Church was led from Constantinople and from here it spread into Russia – Prince Vladimir of Kiev (958–1015) was the first Rus ruler to be baptised. By the 11th century the western Catholic church of Rome and the eastern Orthodox church of Byzantium were irrevocably split. When Constantinople fell to the Turks in 1453, the Russian Orthodox Church and Moscow took the mantle of 'true Church'. A chronicler wrote: 'Two Romes have fallen, but the third stands. And a fourth there shall not

White-walled city

Kremlin (кремль – kreml) is the Russian for a fortress. The word originally meant the sturdiest wood for building. In poetry, Moscow is called 'the white-walled city' – the colour of the 14th-century stone Kremlin walls and the later city walls.

be'. The idea of Moscow as the 'Third Rome' still exerts power over contemporary Russian political thinking.

In this role as home of the true church, under Ivan III (the Great, 1462–1505) and his successor, Vasily III (1505–33), Moscow began to gather other principalities under its rule. This 'gathering of the Rus' was achieved through alliances and conquests, with the covert and sometimes overt support of the Mongol khans.

Perhaps the khans didn't foresee the consequences

St George, adopted by the tsar

of these moves or were simply unable to maintain their enormous conquests. In 1480 Ivan III renounced allegiance to the khan, and by 1493 he had crowned himself Sovereign of All Russia. Having married the daughter of the last Byzantine emperor, he added Byzantium's double-headed eagle to the image of St George as the ruling symbol. His grandson, Ivan IV – Ivan the Terrible – had himself crowned Tsar (Caesar) of All Russia in 1547. By 1556 he had routed the Golden Horde.

Ivan the Terrible established many of Russia's first state institutions and created its first special police, the *oprichniki*. As madness set in, he unleashed them against anyone he feared: boyars (noblemen), citizens, entire towns and villages. He struck and killed his oldest son and heir in 1581, then died just three years later.

The 1628 Old English Court where visiting traders lodged

When Ivan's second son, Fyodor, died in 1598, he left no heir. The council of boyars elected Boris Godunov as tsar, but his reign was marked by crop failures, famine and unrest. The Poles decided to make use of the instability, and put forward a young man claiming to be the first son of Ivan the Terrible. Led by this 'False Dmitry', the Poles invaded Russia and occupied the Kremlin. For eight years the country went through a period of lawlessness and a number of leaders (including another False Dmitry). The invaders were finally routed by a volunteer army led by a meat trader, Kuzma Minin, and Prince Dmitry Pozharsky. This period of chaos and lawlessness is called the Time of Troubles, and ever since it has haunted Russians, who have come to believe that the hand of a strong, even autocratic, leader is better than no hand at all.

THE FIRST ROMANOVS

In 1613 a gathering of boyars, clergy and ranking service gentry met to decide on a new leader. They chose a young boyar named Mikhail Romanov, the first in a dynasty that would last until 1917. In the 17th century Moscow enjoyed a period of relative calm. The city was prosperous and grand, filled with churches, taverns and markets, its bearded, pious citizens clothed in long caftans trimmed with fur. Markets were filled with the chatter of dozens of foreign languages. Peasant women worked at market stalls, but noblemen rarely appeared on the streets: they stayed secluded in their homes.

And then came the Romanov who would be called Peter the Great. Traumatised by a rebellion that took the lives of his family, Peter had largely grown up on the outskirts of the capital. A huge man, some 2m (6ft 7in) tall, with enormous energy, curiosity and a keen mind, he set off to Europe incognito to study the crafts, arts, sciences and state institutions of his European neighbours.

After putting down several rebellions instigated by his older half-sister, Sophia, Peter took control of Russia, crowning himself Emperor and beginning a series of reforms to bring Russia into the prevailing traditions of European civilisation and away from its Asian influences. In 1703 he expanded Russia to the north, building a port on the boggy land straddling the Neva River in the Gulf of Finland. In 1712, he moved the court to his dazzling new city of St Petersburg, named after his patron saint, and declared it the capital of the Russian Empire.

The Poles occupy Moscow during the Time of Troubles

BURNING OF THE CITY

In 1812 Napoleon's Grand Army reached Moscow and entered the Kremlin after the indecisive battle of nearby Borodino. The city's governor had ordered the city to be set on fire and the citizens evacuated. Three-quarters of Moscow's structures were destroyed. Cold and hunger forced Napoleon to retreat. But by the mid-19th century, the rebuilt city was a metropolis of

HOW THE CITY TOOK SHAPE

Moscow began as a small walled fortress in a series of concentric circles intersected by the 'spokes' of roads leading to neighbouring principalities. The Kremlin's first walls were built by Prince Yuri Dolgoruky in 1156. In 1340 Ivan Kalita built sturdier oak walls, reinforced with stucco, which Prince Dmitry Donskoy replaced 27 years later with the white stone walls.

Ivan III – Ivan the Great – invited Italian builders to expand the Kremlin and surround it with the crenellated brick walls (1485–95) that still stand. A few years later a wide, deep moat was dug along the Kremlin walls on Red Square. The next Ivan – Ivan the Terrible – built the second walled city of Kitay-gorod in 1535–38. During the reign of his son, Fyodor, a third circle of walls was built, marked today by the Boulevard Ring Road. In the 17th century, wooden walls were built around the Earthen City, now the Garden Ring Road, enclosing the small settlements of merchants and craftsmen that flourished outside the White City walls.

In the 18th century, the walls were taken down, the moat on Red Square was filled in and the Neglinnaya River was routed underground.

In 1935 under Stalin's first General Plan for the city, streets were broadened, neighbourhoods of crooked lanes were razed and replaced by wide avenues. But the city's fundamental circular structure has not changed. Today there are three main ring roads encircling the city, and a final circular highway that marks the outer city limits.

contrasts: rickety tenements and middle-class apartment buildings, rank outdoor markets and beautifully landscaped public parks, rowdy taverns and elegant restaurants. The 'merchant kings' of commerce began to invest in private and public housing and became generous patrons of the arts. St Petersburg's hold on artistic and cultural life was slowly broken, and Moscow's ballet, conservatory, opera and theatre challenged the best of its northern neighbour, and of Europe's capitals, too.

Lenin comes to power, in Red Square, 1917

REVOLUTION

Russia entered World War I, in which it suffered enormous losses. Poverty-stricken, weary and deprived, the population reached the end of its patience. In February 1917 the last tsar, Nicholas II, abdicated, and was succeeded by a Provisional Government. Vladimir Lenin and his revolutionaries seized the moment, and on 25 October 1917 they claimed power. The tsar and his family were murdered. Lenin moved the capital back to Moscow in 1918, although it was officially designated the capital of the USSR only in 1922 when the Civil War between the White and Red Russians ended.

RED MOSCOW

Slowly Moscow began to change. Manor houses were turned into state buildings, churches were destroyed or

Soviet communist propaganda poster. The caption reads: 'Glory to Stalin, the great architect of communism!'

converted into warehouses, museums, offices and dormitories; shops were expropriated; one-family dwellings turned into communal apartments. In the 1930s, the General Plan began to reshape Moscow into the city we know today.

Work was halted when Hitler's troops attacked the USSR on 22 June 1941. During World War II, 20 million Russian lives were lost and much of the country's agricultural and industrial might was destroyed. Moscow did not suffer as much as other Soviet cities in bombing raids, and most of the city's artistic and historical treasures were evacuated east.

Buoyed for decades by high oil prices and scientific breakthroughs, the Soviet economy provided the bare essentials and some luxuries. There were no slums and little crime; incomes were low, but so were prices. By the Brezhnev era, the purges and terror of the Stalinist years had stopped, even if artistic, intellectual and political dissent were stifled. Few citizens could travel abroad, but most could take employer-sponsored holidays to the Black Sea coast. Discontent was muttered in kitchens, but not on the streets.

END OF THE SOVIET ERA

That all changed when Mikhail Gorbachev came to power in 1985. Determined to resurrect the failing economy, he proposed a policy of openness, *perestroika*, and economic acceleration. But his policies were both too little and too late. Once the door was opened to honest appraisal of the country's system, unrest began to rise.

The old guard tried to stem the tide of incipient revolution in August 1991 when they attempted to depose Gorbachev, but enough people came out on the streets – and enough army units refused to fight the demonstrators – for the coup to fail.

Former Soviet republics declared independence. In December 1991 the presidents of three republics, Russia, Ukraine and Belarus, met outside Minsk to formally disband the USSR. On 25 December 1991 Mikhail Gorbachev resigned as President of the Soviet Union. That evening the red Soviet flag was lowered over the Kremlin and the Russian tricolour was raised.

The transition from the Soviet system to a modern, capitalist economy has not been easy. Boris Yeltsin inherited a country that was bankrupt and economically backward, with almost no modern legal or political institutions. After a second bloodier coup attempt in 1993, power was consolidated in the president's hands. But economic progress was fraught with hyperinflation, factory and collective farm closings, and illegal privatisation. The population lost their savings three times in less than a decade. Citizens blamed

Yeltsin for their troubles, and few were sorry when he resigned on New Year's Eve 1999.

THE MODERN CITY

Vladimir Putin, a former KGB officer, was elected in president in 2000 and again in 2004. The Russian constitution prevented Putin from having a third consecutive term, so before the 2008 elections, he nominated Dmitry Medvedev as his successor. Medvedev was elected president and the next day he appointed Putin his prime minister and transferred political power back to him. During the Putin-Medvedev era, Russia has enjoyed relative stability and economic growth; despite attracting criticism for limiting press freedoms, curbing political diversity and repealing direct election of governors and mayors, Putin and Medvedev have been widely praised for restoring order in the country and enhancing Russia's role in the world. In 2012, Putin once again won the presidential election. All four parties in the State Duma support Putin, so in recent years the Duma has become little more than a rubber stamp, as Putin effectively rules by decree. In 2014, Russia annexed Crimea from Ukraine, which started a military conflict that is ongoing at the time of writing in 2016.

Guarding the Tomb of the Unknown Soldier

The capital city of Moscow, however, has journeyed through a hundred years of history in just two decades. It has emerged as a bustling, modern European capital and the centre of the Russian government. It is also a major culture and business hub, and is continuing to grow at a very fast pace.

HISTORICAL LANDMARKS

1147 First mention of Moscow in the chronicles.

1237–40 Mongols invade Russia, destroying Moscow and other cities.

1480 Ivan III renounces allegiance to the khan.

1485–95 Current brick walls built around the Kremlin.

1547–56 Ivan the Terrible defeats the Golden Horde.

1605–13 The Time of Troubles.

1712 Peter the Great moves the capital to St Petersburg.

1812 Napoleon's troops enter Moscow.

1825 Bolshoy Theatre is opened.

1861 Serfdom is abolished.

1905 Strikes and workers' uprisings.

1917 Soviet power is proclaimed; government moves to Moscow.

1922 The USSR is established with Moscow as its capital.

1924 Death of Lenin.

1935 First metro line is opened.

1935 The first General Plan for Moscow's reconstruction.

1941–5 The Great Patriotic War; 20 million Russians die.

1947–53 Construction of Stalin's 'Seven Sisters'.

1953 Death of Stalin.

1961 Yuri Gagarin becomes first man in space.

1985 Mikhail Gorbachev becomes leader with *perestroika* policy.

1991 Gorbachev resigns as President of the Soviet Union; Boris Yeltsin is elected President of the Russian Federation.

1992 Yuri Luzhkov becomes mayor.

1998 Economic crisis.

2002 Chechen fighters storm Palace of Culture theatre.

2008 Dmitry Medvedev elected president.

2010 Sergei Sobyanin appointed mayor.

2012 Vladimir Putin wins the presidential election.

2014 Russia intervenes in eastern Ukraine and annexes Crimea. Moscow's population exceeds 12 million.

2015 Liberal politician Boris Nemtsov is assassinated in Moscow.

2018 Moscow to host the FIFA World Cup Final.

WHERE TO GO

Moscow retains the basic layout of an ancient Russian city: a *kremlin* (fortress) in the centre surrounded by a series of concentric ring roads, with the main thoroughfares out of the city like spokes in these wheels. For the purpose of this guide, we have divided the city into sections, like pieces of pie, with the narrow tip near the Kremlin and the rest expanding in a large triangle towards the outskirts of the city.

Most sights are within the boundaries of the Garden Ring road and can be visited on foot. For sights outside the Garden Ring, or to start at a point far from your hotel, use the metro – the fastest way to get around, and with stations that are sights in themselves (see page 13). For a trip out of the city, consider a tour agency or freelance guide with car and driver.

Moscow's wealth of art museums, extraordinary religious and civil architecture, historical and cultural sites are daunting to the tourist with just a few days in the city. As you plan your day, be sure to leave time to do some wandering: stroll along the tree-shaded Boulevard Ring or the crooked little lanes of the older city, enter tiny churches overshadowed by apartment and business buildings, slip into courtyards and see grandmothers chatting on a bench while children play in a sandbox, have a coffee or enjoy a cone of rich ice cream. Stop and look around. You're sure to see ghosts of Moscow's past – a *style moderne* apartment building, a crumbling manor house wall, a forgotten bust of a revolutionary hero – peeking into the modern world of neon lights, fast-food, mobile phones and pop music. Catch it while you can.

The Red Square and Mausoleum of Lenin

THE KREMLIN

The spiritual, artistic and ruling heart of Russia is the **Kremlin ❶** – a 27.5-hectare (68-acre) triangle of land set on a high bluff overlooking the Moscow River. The original Kremlin was a self-contained city with dwellings, churches, traders and artisans. Over the years, the walls were rebuilt and the territory expanded. In 1937, the two-headed eagles that were the symbol of the imperial Romanov family were taken down and replaced by Communist red stars. The Kremlin is still the residence of the President and his administration.

The fortress's **red wall** is 2.2km (1.4 miles) long, and has 20 towers and four entrances: the Spasskaya (Saviour), Borovitskaya, Troitskaya (Trinity) and Nikolskaya. The clock on the Saviour Gates was installed in 1625 when English architect Christopher Halloway redesigned the tower. After the 1917 Revolution, its tune changed from a patriotic march to the *Internationale*. The oldest tower is the Taynitskaya, built in 1485; the newest is the small Tsarskaya (Tsar's) tower, built in 1680, where Ivan the Terrible supposedly watched over his city. The tallest is the Trinity (80m/262ft), once connected by a drawbridge stretching over the Neglinnaya River to the Kutafya Tower. This is now the **main entrance** for visitors (tel: 495-697 0349 and 495-695 4146; www.kreml.ru; Fri–Wed 10am–6pm; separate tickets must be purchased for the State Armoury Palace Museum; pre-book guided tours in English at travel agencies).

Not all the buildings can be visited. The **Arsenal** (1736), the classical **Senate**, built by Russian architect Matvey Kazakov in 1776–87 (now the President's residence) and the **Presidium**,

On parade

In warm weather, on all but the last Saturday of the month, the Kremlin Horse Guards perform in Cathedral Square at noon. On the last Saturday of the month they put on a display in Red Square.

another administration building, are all off limits to tourists, while the **State Kremlin Palace**, the newest building (1959–61), designed for Party Congresses, is now a 6,000-seat venue for ballet, opera and concerts.

The area open to visitors is around and within the magnificent Cathedral Square (see page 30). On the perimeter is the **Patriarch's Palace and Church of the Twelve Apostles** (Патриаршие палаты и Церковь Двенадцати апостолов; Patriarshie palaty i Tserkov Dvenadtsati apostolov). The Patriarch's Palace was built in 1656 for the head of the Russian Orthodox Church and is now the Museum of 17th-Century Life and Applied Art.

Outside the palace is the 40-tonne **Tsar Cannon**. Designed to defend the Saviour Gates, it was used only once, to fire the False Dmitry's remains towards the west after the Poles were defeated.

The Kremlin on the Moscow River

Frescoes inside the Dormition Cathedral

Near the cannon is the magnificent **Ivan the Great Bell Tower** (Колокольня Ивана Великого, Kolokolnya Ivana Velikovo), named after the church of St John (Ivan) Climacus that once stood on this spot. It has two tiers (built in 1508 and 1600) and stands 81m (266ft) high. The adjacent Assumption Belfry was added in 1543, and the annex was commissioned in 1642. The 21 bells, including the 64-tonne Resurrection or Festival bell, are rung on special occasions.

The 200-tonne **Tsar Bell** beside the tower is, like the Tsar Cannon, a monument to an obsession with size. It was still in its casting pit when fire swept the Kremlin. Cold water was thrown on the still-hot bell to stop it melting, and an 11-tonne chunk broke off, so it could never be used.

CATHEDRAL SQUARE

With three remarkable cathedrals, **Cathedral Square ❷** is the ceremonial heart of the Kremlin. Each had a special role in the life of the imperial family. The oldest, grandest and the most important is the **Dormition Cathedral** (Успенский собор, Uspensky sobor, sometimes called the Cathedral of the Assumption). Built in 1475–79 by Alberti Fiorovanti of Bologna, this was where tsars were crowned. Entry is via a magnificent portal, with 17th-century frescoes and carved doors brought from the monastic city of Suzdal in 1401.

Frescoes and icons illuminate the interior. The five-tiered iconostasis dates from 1652, but some of its icons were made as early as the 14th century. Tombs of the church leaders, metropolitans and patriarchs line the walls. The Monomakh Throne was installed for Ivan the Terrible in 1551; its carvings show scenes from the life of Vladimir Monomakh (1053–1125), the popular grand prince of Ancient Rus. During the Napoleonic invasion, the French army used the cathedral as a stable.

Tucked between the cathedral and the Faceted Palace (see page 33) is the small **Church of the Deposition of the Robe** (Церковь Ризоположения, Tserkov Rizopolozheniya), built by Pskov architects in 1484–86. Once the private chapel of patriarchs and metropolitans, it now houses a small collection of wooden religious sculpture.

Facing the Dormition Cathedral on the other side of the square is the **Cathedral of the Archangel** (Архангельский

INSIDE AN ORTHODOX CHURCH

In Orthodox churches a screen of icons called an iconostasis separates the main, 'earthly' part of the church from the sanctuary. The lowest tier of icons, the Local tier with local saints, has Royal Doors through which the priests enter and leave the sanctuary. The second tier is the Deisis and has an icon of Christ in the centre. Above it is the Feast Day tier, with scenes from the life of Christ and Mary. The fourth tier is the Prophet's tier with images of saints who foretold the coming of Christ. The final tier is the Patriarch's tier, with icons of the first Church fathers. Simple churches might have only one tier; some large cathedrals have nine. Icons and frescoes tell the story of Christianity and most churches have an image of the Last Judgment over the entry, so worshippers coming into the church, pass from 'sin and damnation' towards the soaring light of the heavens in the cupola and images of salvation at the altar.

The domes above Cathedral Square

собор, Arkhangelsky sobor), the final resting place for the early tsars. It was commissioned in 1505 by Ivan III to replace an older church, and built by the Milanese architect Alevisio Novo, who incorporated Western ornamentation, such as the scalloping on the gables and Corinthian capitals. The frescoes date from 1652–60. The original iconostasis was destroyed by the French in 1812 and the present one installed in 1813. The tsars were interred in this church from 1340 until 1712, when the capital was moved to St Petersburg. Mikhail Romanov, first tsar in the Romanov dynasty, is here, as is Ivan the Terrible, although his tomb behind the iconostasis is not visible.

The neighbouring, golden-domed **Annunciation Cathedral** (Благовещенский собор, Blagoveshchensky sobor) was built in 1489 by architects from the ancient city of Pskov and reconstructed so many times it seems a confusing jumble of cupolas. Its frescoes are mainly by the monk Feodosius (1508) but its iconostasis is from a previous church on this site built in the 1360s and considered one of the finest in Russia. Its icons were painted by three of Russia's great icon-painters: Theophanes the Greek (c.1340–1410), Andrei Rublyov (1360–1430) and Prokhor of Gorodets, Rublyov's teacher. The cathedral served as the private church of tsars and grand princes. The extended porch and Ivan the Terrible Steps were built to allow Ivan to attend services without entering the church after a penance was imposed for his many marriages.

THE KREMLIN PALACES

Between Cathedral Square and the Borovitskaya Gate are three palaces that combined the living and reception quarters for the imperial family, which are now connected under one roof. The most striking is the **Faceted Palace** (Гранитовая палата, Granitovaya palata), named after its patterned façade and built in 1491 by Italians Marco Ruffo and Pietro Solario as one of the main administrative buildings for the tsar. The upper floor is one enormous chamber lavishly painted with historical and Biblical scenes, where the tsar held audiences.

Leading down to Cathedral Square is the Red or Beautiful Staircase by which the tsars entered Cathedral Square, and where in 1682 young Peter the Great saw his relatives murdered. The staircase was demolished by Stalin but rebuilt to the original plans under Boris Yeltsin.

Attached to the Faceted Palace is the **Great Kremlin Palace** ❸ (Большой Кремлёвский дворец, Bolshoy Kremlyovsky dvorets), the imposing yellow-and-white building overlooking the river. It was built in the reign of Nicholas I by the Russian architect Konstantin Ton, and served as the residence of the imperial family during their visits to Moscow. The family residence was on

Palace tours

Tours of the Kremlin's palaces by foreigners can be arranged only through Patriarshy Dom; tel: 495-795 0927. They take place about twice a month.

Crowns of state in the Armoury

the ground floor (where the current president's chambers are); several lavishly decorated reception and meeting halls are on the upper floor.

The third palace is the **Terem Palace** (Теремной дворец, Teremnoy dvorets), built in 1635 by Russian architects and restored in 1837. A wonderfully evocative building, it has low-vaulted ceilings covered with ornamentation and a magnificent Throne Room.

ARMOURY PALACE MUSEUM AND DIAMOND FUND

The **State Armoury Palace Museum** ❹ (Оружейная палата, Oruzheynaya palata) was established as a workshop in 1511. The current Armoury building by Konstantin Ton (1844–51) houses a sumptuous collection of works that celebrate Russia's imperial heritage. It includes ceremonial armoury, tsars' personal effects, thrones, Fabergé eggs and the sacred vestments of the church. The collection contains a number of crowns, most importantly the Crown of Monomakh, traditionally believed to have been given to the first Christian Rus leader, Grand Prince Vladimir of Kiev, by his father-in-law, Constantine XI, the last emperor of Byzantium.

The **Diamond Fund** ❺ (Алмазный фонд, Almazny fond; Fri–Wed 10am–5pm with a break from 1–2pm, tours in Russian every 20 minutes with an English written brochure) displays the imperial jewels, including Catherine the Great's coronation crown, the 190-carat Orlov diamond, the 89-carat Shah diamond, and diamond-encrusted victory orders awarded to Stalin's marshals.

RED SQUARE AND ENVIRONS

For most of its history, the vast, empty expanse (700m by 130m/2,300ft by 425ft) of **Red Square** ❻ (Красная площадь, Krasnaya ploshchad) alongside the Kremlin was a teeming hive of traders, gossips and townspeople, covered with vendors' huts and bustling with business from morning till night.

The main entry is on the north side, through the **Resurrection (or Iberian) Gate** ❼ (Воскресенские ворота, Voskresenskiye vorota) from Manège Square. The gate was originally part of the Kitay-gorod wall built in 1538 to enclose this area of traders. Its chapel held the icon of the Iberian Mother of God, and before entering the Kremlin

St Basil's Cathedral

tsars and emperors would stop to honour this miracle-working image. Stalin had the gate torn down in 1931, but the structure was rebuilt to the original plans in 1996. On the pavement in front of the gate is the 'kilometre zero' marker from which all distances in Russia were measured.

On the right as you enter the square is the **State Historical Museum** ❽ (Государственный исторический музей, Gosudarstvenny istorichesky muzey; Sun–Thu 10am–6pm, Fri–Sat until 9pm; English language audio players available for hire) built in 1874–83 in the Russian Revival style with turrets, gables and towers. Selections from the large collection narrate the history of Russia from the Stone Age to the 19th century in profusely decorated halls.

Opposite is the pink **Kazan Cathedral** ❾ (Казанский собор, Kazansky sobor; daily 8am–8pm) built in 1636 to house the Kazan Mother of God icon and celebrate victory over the Poles. Torn down by Stalin in 1936, it was rebuilt in 1993 and is a popular place to stop and worship.

Dominating the east side of the square is **GUM** ❿, the State Department Store (daily 10am–10pm). This beautiful airy marketplace was called the Upper Trading Rows when built in 1890–93 in the Russian Revival style. It is now filled with foreign and Russian shops, eateries, and a kitschy faux Stalin-era food shop called Gastronom #1. From late November to mid-March, there is an ice skating rink next to GUM on Red Square (daily, 10am–midnight; skate rental available).

Facing GUM, in front of the Kremlin, is the **Mausoleum of V.I. Lenin** ⓫ (Мавзолей

Kilometre zero

To make sure you return to Moscow, stand with your back to the 'kilometre zero' marker by the Resurrection Gate and toss a coin over your shoulder. If it lands on the marker, you're sure to come back again.

В.И. Ленина, Mavzoley V.I. Lenina; Tue–Thu, Sat 10am–1pm; closed for long periods for treatment of Lenin's body; free), where the first leader of the USSR lies in state, preserved by a unique process. Stalin's body was placed behind the mausoleum by the Kremlin wall after his death in 1953, and his name added over the entrance. His body and name were removed in 1961.

ST BASIL'S CATHEDRAL
At the far end of the square is **St Basil's Cathedral**  (Храм Василия Блаженного,

St Basil's Cathedral at night

Khram Vasiliya Blazhennovo; summer Thu–Tue 10am–7pm, shorter hours in winter; English language excursions available tel: 495-698 3304), Russia's most famous landmark, rising in a fairground swirl of bright colours and fanciful forms. Commissioned by Ivan the Terrible to commemorate the Russian victory over the Golden Horde in 1556, its full name is the Cathedral of the Intercession by the Moat, which once flowed by the Kremlin walls here. It became known as St Basil's in honour of a holy man whom the tsar befriended and whose remains were interred in a separate chapel added to the cathedral.

Inside, the cathedral is not one large space, but nine small churches linked by covered passageways decorated in profuse and brightly coloured geometric and floral designs.

In front of St Basil's is a **statue to Pozharsky and Minin**, by Ivan Martos (1818), the prince and meat trader who led the forces that drove out the Polish invaders in 1612.

Near the church is **Lobnoe Mesto** (the 'place of the brow'), a round stone platform dating from 1534; the current podium faced with white stone was made in 1786. On this spot state proclamations were read, religious ceremonies held and once a year the tsar appeared before the people.

KITAY-GOROD

The area north-east of Red Square that stretches from GUM to New and Old Squares is called Kitay-gorod. In 1538 the area was enclosed by a 6-m (20-ft) thick wall with 14 towers, to make a second fortified city. This was the main trade district of old Moscow: streets filled with shops and markets, tenements, taverns and trading houses – as well as four monasteries and 18 churches. In the late 19th and early 20th centuries, elegant shopping centres, banks, insurance companies and the stock exchange were built on the narrow streets. In Soviet times much of the area was taken over by government buildings.

A man clutching a portrait of Vladimir Lenin

Today **Nikolskaya ulitsa**, running back from the northern corner of Red Square, is the prime shopping street, and many of the buildings are taken up by various ministries and higher courts. But gems of architectural beauty and rare museums hide among the office buildings.

Chambers in Zaryade, birthplace of the first Romanov tsar

On **Ulitsa Vavarka**, at the southern end of Red Square, part of what was once called Zaryade ('beyond the rows' of traders' booths on Red Square), are several lovely churches and ancient structures (marred by current construction on the site of the former huge Rossiya Hotel, which was demolished in 2006). The **Old English Court** (Палаты старого английского двора, Palaty starovo angliyskovo dvora; Ulitsa Varvarka 4a; Tue–Wed, Fri–Sun 10am–8pm, Thu 11pm–9pm; closed last Fri of the month) was erected in 1628 to house visiting merchants and dignitaries from England. An exhibition narrates the history of relations between the two countries.

Further down the street is the small museum called the **Chambers in Zaryade** ⓭ (Музей Палаты в Зарядье, Muzey Palaty v Zaryade; Ulitsa Varvarka 10; Thu–Mon 10am–5pm, Wed 11am–7pm; closed first Mon of the month) where the first Romanov tsar, Mikhail, was born in 1596. It is a beautifully reconstructed medieval Russian dwelling, with low-vaulted ceilings, deep-set mica windows, chased leather 'wallpaper' and a *terem*, a section on the top floor of the house where women were secluded.

On the opposite side of the street is the **Old Merchants' Quarters** (Старый Гостиный двор, Stary Gostiny dvor) that housed booths of visiting traders. Rebuilt many times, the current structure was recently restored with an exhibition space, shops and offices.

BEYOND KITAY-GOROD

The central street of Kitay-gorod, ulitsa Ilinka, starts at **Red Square** and ends between **Old Square** (towards the river) and **New Square** (towards Lubyanka Square). **Old Square** now houses the Presidential Administration. The neighbourhood to the east of the boulevard is called **Ivanovskaya gora** – 'John's Hill' – after St John's Convent, which is located there. It is a charming area full of winding streets, manor houses, little squares and churches, including the restored **Choral Synagogue** (Московская хоральная синагога, Moskovskaya khoralnaya sinagoga) at Spasoglinishchevsky pereulok 10, built in the classical style and opened in 1906.

Southeast of here is the **Museum of the Cold War** – aka **Bunker 42** (Музей Холодной войны, Muzey Kholodnoy voiny, 5 Kotelnichesky pereulok 11; www.bunker42.com; daily 10am–7pm). This 7,000 square metre (75,347 sq ft) facility, located 65m (213ft) underground near the Taganskaya metro station, was built in the 1950s and maintained until the 21st century as a bunker for the leadership in case of nuclear war. Now it is a museum, with tours (about $43 for an English tour, usually held every day at various times, to book call tel: 499-703 4455) that include a thrilling enactment of a nuclear strike.

THREE SQUARES

The great expanse to the west of Red Square was once a boggy lowland filled with tenements, taverns and huts selling moss (used to insulate wooden houses), hunters' bounty and pre-Revolutionary fast food (meat pies and other savouries). Cleared during one of the first Soviet urban renewals and rebuilt with several imposing state buildings, it has been undergoing another major renovation since the USSR fell.

MANÈGE SQUARE

The broad space in front of the Resurrection Gate is **Manège Square** (Манежная площадь, Manezhnaya ploshchad) with the equestrian statue of **Marshal Zhukov**, a World War II hero. In the centre of the square is a smart underground mall, with restaurants, called **Okhotny**

Manège exhibition hall, which was built as a riding school

Ryad (Hunters' Row; daily 10am–10pm), a popular haunt when the weather is bad. The mall and park above it were designed by Zurab Tsereteli, former Mayor Luzhkov's favourite artist. A part of the Neglinnaya River has been released above ground to flow amid sculptures of fairy tale characters and fountains during the summer months.

Beside it, beneath the Kremlin walls, are the **Aleksandrovsky Gardens**, landscaped when the Neglinnaya River was routed underground in 1821. There you can visit the **Tomb of the Unknown Soldier**, dedicated in 1967 on the 25th anniversary of the Battle of Moscow under an eternal flame. A **Grotto**, also called the 'Ruins', is built into the Kremlin walls and an obelisk dedicated in 1913 to the 300th anniversary of the Romanov dynasty was later transformed into the Monument to Revolutionary Thinkers.

The world-famous Bolshoy Theatre, rebuilt and renovated several times during its history

Beside the gardens is the **Manège**, a neo-classical yellow structure with white columns that gives its name to the square. Built as a riding school in 1817, it is now the Central Exhibition Hall.

On the far side of Manège Square is the yellow façade of **Moscow State University**, one of Russia's finest neo-classical buildings. It was built by Matvey Kazakov in 1793 and rebuilt after 1812. The 'new building' of the university, from 1836, is on the other side of Bolshaya Nikitskaya ulitsa.

On the corner of Tverskaya ulitsa, the city's main commercial street (see page 45), is the elegant 1903 **National Hotel**, which served as the First House of Soviets (living quarters for the government) in 1918.

The imposing grey building on the opposite corner of Tverskaya housed the State Planning Committee until 1992; now it is the **State Duma**, the lower house of parliament.

REVOLUTION SQUARE

Revolution Square, north of the Resurrection Gate, saw fighting during the Bolshevik uprising. The turreted red-brick building, once the Lenin Museum, holds temporary shows. Opposite is the small underground **Archaeological Museum** (Музей археологии Москвы, Muzey arkheologii Moskvy; Manezhnaya ploshchad 1A; Tue–Wed, Fri–Sun 10am–8pm, Thu 11pm–9pm, closed last Fri of the month), with artefacts dating back to the 12th century found during the excavations of Manège Square. In the centre of the square is the Moskva Hotel, a new facsimile of a Stalin-era structure.

Tverskaya ulitsa

THEATRE SQUARE

Revolution Square stretches across into **Theatre Square**, dedicated to the city's two main theatres, the Bolshoy (Grand) and Maly (Small) theatres, and improbably overseen by the boxy statue of Karl Marx in the centre. On the eastern side of the square is the elegantly renovated **Metropol Hotel**, built 1899–1903 by the Russian-born English architect William Walcott. On the north wall is the mosaic 'The Princess of Dreams', by the artist Mikhail Vrubel.

Behind the hotel is one of the original Kitay-gorod towers and the **Tretyakov Passage** to Nikolskaya ulitsa, built by the philanthropic Tretyakov brothers in 1862. Today it is filled with luxury shops.

The **Bolshoy Theatre**, founded in 1776, became the Great Imperial Theatre in 1805. Burnt and redesigned many times, the present façade, with a statue of Apollo in his chariot, was erected in 1853.

The **Maly Theatre** to the right of the Bolshoy was the premier drama theatre in the 19th and early 20th centuries. Just beyond it is the TsUM store (see page 50).

West of the Bolshoy along ulitsa Okhotny Ryad is the pale-green classical **Hall of Unions**, built in the 1770s as the Club of the Russian Nobility and today a concert and events venue.

TVERSKAYA ULITSA & THE NORTHWEST

Moscow's main street is Tverskaya ulitsa, filled with shops, restaurants and crowds all day and night. Parallel to Tverskaya ulitsa are Bolshaya Nikitskaya, Dmitrovka and Petrovka, each street with its own charms and sights.

TVERSKAYA ULITSA

Tverskaya ulitsa ⑭ was the road to the nearby principality of Tver, which was extended to the new capital in St Petersburg. Since tsars and tsarinas used this road when they came to the ancient capital for coronations and official visits, it was called the 'Tsar's Road'. In the 1930s it was broadened from 18m/60ft to 60m/200ft. Important buildings were moved back and others demolished, and many neo-classical Stalinist apartment buildings erected. Today it is the city's busiest commercial street and the site of many civic and cultural events.

First on the right, up from Manège Square is the pedestrianised **Kamergersky pereulok**, one of the city's most lively spots, especially during the warm months when its outdoor cafés beckon. At No. 5 is the elegant *style moderne* **Moscow Art Theatre**, designed by Fyodor Shekhtel in 1902. The sculpture over the right door reflects the seagull that became the theatre's emblem in honour of Chekhov's play, *The Seagull*. The theatre contains the small but interesting **MKhAT Museum** (Музей МХАТа им. А.П.

Tretyakov legacy

The Tretyakov family was one of the richest in pre-Revolutionary Russia. Two brothers, Pavel and Sergey, were philanthropists and patrons of the arts. Pavel's collection of Russian paintings was the foundation of the Tretyakov Gallery (see page 75). Sergey willed his collection of Western European art to the city of Moscow and it is now part of the Pushkin Museum of Fine Arts (see page 53).

Чехова, Muzey MKhATa im. AP Chekhova; Kamergersky pereulok 3a; Wed–Sun 11am–6pm).

Further up Tverskaya, on the eastern side, is the equestrian statue to Moscow's founder, **Yury Dolgoruky**, erected in 1954, looking stolid and facing the red, classical Mayor's Office. Built by Kazakov in 1782 as the home of the governors-general of Moscow, it has been rebuilt several times.

At No. 14 Tverskaya visitors can step back in time to enjoy pre-Revolutionary splendour at **Yeliseev's Emporium** ⓯. Once a famous literary salon, the building was purchased by the Yeliseev family in 1898 and turned into a magnificent *style moderne* food shop. Although it was given the proletarian name of Gastronom No. 1 during the Soviet years, it always had a few rare delicacies.

PUSHKIN SQUARE AND ENVIRONS

Pushkin Square ⓰ marks the intersection of the Boulevard Ring with Tverskaya ulitsa. Once surrounded by churches and monasteries, today it is filled with restaurants, cafés and shops, the country's largest film theatre and the biggest McDonald's, advertised with bright neon. The monument to the poet Alexander Pushkin (1799–1837) that gave the square its name is a favourite meeting spot, where earnest men holding bouquets wait for their sweethearts. It is also the site of political rallies, which often close the square at weekends.

Architecturally, the square and environs have some interesting sights. The **Izvestiya building** (1927) is a fine example of Constructivism. At nearby Nastasinsky pereulok 3 is the blue faceted Russian Revival **Old Treasury building** (1913–16). On Malaya Dmitrovka is the lovely, ornate **Church of the Nativity of the Mother of God in Putinki**. This was the last 'tent' church built in Moscow; in 1653, the year after it was completed, Patriarch Nikon banned the style, claiming it was too secular and too cramped inside due to the thick walls necessary to support the spire.

For a primer in modern Russian history visit the **Museum of Modern Russian History** (Музей современной истории России, Muzey sovremennoy istorii Rossii; www.sovrhistory.ru; Tue–Wed and Fri–Sun 11am–7pm, Thu noon–9pm, closed last Fri of the month) back on Tverskaya ulitsa at No. 21. This mansion was turned into the English Nobleman's Club in 1831. After 1918 it opened as the Museum of the Revolution. It has a replica of the English Club's famous library, a fascinating exhibition of Soviet posters and gifts to Stalin, as well as comprehensive exhibits of Russia's tumultuous Revolutionary and post-Revolutionary history, bringing the story right up to date. A large screen shows films of the city in the early 20th century.

Clearing snow off Pushkin Square

TRIUMFALNAYA SQUARE

Between Pushkin Square and Tverskaya Zastava, Tverskaya ulitsa is lined with clothes shops, hotels, fast-food outlets and top restaurants. The square after Pushkin Square was renamed **Triumfalnaya** in the 1990s, but is still commonly called 'Mayakovka' in reference to the statue of the poet Vladimir Mayakovsky (1893–1930) that dominates the space.

Behind the statue are the ornamented Stalinist towers of the **Peking Hotel.** On the south side of the square are the famous **Tchaikovsky Concert Hall** and the **Satirical Theatre**. If you walk through the tall wrought-iron gates next to the theatre, you'll find yourself in a pleasant haven of peace called the **Aquarium Gardens**, which opened in 1893 as the Chicago Gardens. The

STALIN'S 'SEVEN SISTERS'

It's difficult for non-Muscovites to orient themselves in the city. The Moscow River snakes through the centre with such an enormous loop, you can be both north and south of the river at the same time. Then there are seven 'Stalinist skyscrapers' that look similar, making you wonder if you are on the Sparrow Hills or the Arbat. The 'seven sisters' were ordered by Stalin after World War II to celebrate the victory and the dawning of a more prosperous age. They were designed and built by different architects working under one general vision: a mix inspired by Manhattan's 20th-century skyscrapers (such as the Woolworth Building), neo-classicism and 17th-century Muscovite styles. They are on Kotelnicheskaya Naberezhnaya (Embankment), Kudrinskaya ploschchad (both apartment buildings), Smolenskaya ploshchad (the Ministry of Foreign Affairs) and at Krasnye Vorota (housing two ministries and apartments). There's also the Ukraina and Leningradsky hotels, and Moscow State University on Sparrow Hills. In recent years, an eighth sister was built: the Triumph Palace apartment building at Sokol metro station.

Mossoviet Theatre and Starlite Diner stand on either side of a pretty fountain.

BOLSHAYA NIKITSKAYA ULITSA AND ENVIRONS

Once known as a 'Museum of Classicism' because of its fine buildings, **Bolshaya Nikitskaya ulitsa** starts at Manège Square between the two buildings of Moscow University. Here visitors will find the small and quirky **Zoological Museum** (Зоологический музей московского

Kotelnicheskaya Naberezhnaya, one of the Seven Sisters

университета, Zoologichesky muzey Moskovskovo universiteta, Bolshaya Nikitskaya 6; http://zmmu.msu.ru; Tue–Wed, Fri–Sun 10am–5pm, Thu 1–9pm; closed last Tue of the month), where you can see all kinds of stuffed Russian beasts, birds and sea creatures. Further up the street is a well reconstructed 17th-century house on Bryusov pereulok and the small gem of the **Church of the Little Ascension** at No. 18.

Opposite the church, a statue of Petr Tchaikovsky stands in front of the prestigious **Moscow Tchaikovsky Conservatory** (Московская государственная консерватория им. П.И. Чайковского, Moskovskaya gosudarstvennaya konservatoriya im. PI Chaikovskovo; tel: 495-629 2060; Bolshaya Nikitskaya 13). The conservatory was founded in 1866 by Nikolay Rubenstein, brother of the famous pianist and composer Anton Rubenstein, and is the premiere concert hall in the city. With brilliant acoustics and a pleasant old-world ambiance, it is an ideal place to hear the very best of Russia's concert music.

Petrovsky Passage

Petrovsky Passazh at Petrovka 10 was built in the *style moderne* structure in 1903 as a small and elite shopping arcade; the heroic workers were added to the façade in 1920.

Not far from the conservatory on Leontevsky pereulok is the **Museum of Konstantin Stanislavsky** (Дом-музей К.С. Станиславского, Dom-muzey KS Stanislavskovo, Leontievsky pereulok 6; Wed and Fri noon–7pm, Thu 11am–9pm, Sat–Sun 11am–6pm, closed last Thu of the month), where the actor, director and founder of the method school of acting lived with his wife, the actress Maria Lilina, from the late 1920s to his death in 1948. The apartment, decorated in Stanislavsky's favourite European medieval style, is filled with memorabilia from the Moscow Art Theatre, including stage set models and manuscripts.

BOLSHAYA DMITROVKA AND ULITSA PETROVKA

Parallel to Tverskaya ulitsa on the north side is **Bolshaya Dmitrovka**, which begins at Okhotny Ryad at the Hall of Unions and ends at the Boulevard Ring. This narrow street lined with shops and cafés is constantly clogged with state vehicles trying to get to the Prosecutor General's Offices at No. 15a, and the upper chamber of the Russian Parliament, the Federation Council (No. 26). Off it is another pedestrianised street, **Stoleshnikov pereulok** (Tablecloth Lane, named after weavers who lived here), with high-end shops.

Ulitsa Petrovka, which takes its name from the monastery at the top of the street, begins between the Bolshoy and Maly Theatres at **TsUM** (the Russian acronym for Central Department Store), in what was the Scottish firm of Muir and Mirrielees. The neo-Gothic structure of 1908 is once again a smart department store. Developed after the neighbouring Neglinnaya River was funnelled underground in the 19th century, Petrovka was inhabited by a mix of well-to-do traders, craftsmen and carriage makers.

Just up the street is the small, but haunting **History of the Gulag Museum** ⓱ (Государственный музей истории ГУЛага, Gosudarstvenny muzey istorii gulaga; Petrovka ulitsa 16; www.gmig.ru; Tue–Wed, Fri–Sun 11am–7pm, Thu noon–9pm, closed last Fri of the month). This shows the enormous system of labour camps that covered the USSR. There is little in English, but photographs and memorabilia tell the story eloquently. It includes a chilling reconstruction of camp barracks.

The **Vysoko-Petrovsky Monastery** (Высоко-Петровский монастырь, Vysoko-Petrovsky monastyr; daily 7am–8pm; free) at the end of the street was founded in the reign of Dmitry Donskoy, and first mentioned in the chronicles in 1377.

TsUM central department store

Opposite the monastery is the **Moscow Museum of Contemporary Art** (Московский музей современного искусства, Moskovsky muzey sovremennovo iskusstva; Ulitsa Petrovka 25; www.mmoma.ru; Mon–Wed, Fri–Sun noon–8pm, Thu 1–9pm, closed last Mon of month; English exhibit notes). Founded on the collection of the artist Zurab Tsereteli, this is the first attempt in Moscow to display works of modern art, the 'non-conformist art' of the

Petrovsky Palace

Soviet era, and the schools that have followed. There are wonderful canvases from the early 20th century avant-garde as well as lithographs by Dalí, Picasso and Léger.

As Petrovka continues across the boulevard, its name changes into **Karetny Ryad** (Carriage Row). At No. 3 is a charming pocket park, **Hermitage Garden**, opened in 1894, where the first film was shown in Russia. Now filled with cafés, it is a venue for concerts and music festivals.

BEYOND THE RING ROAD

On the other side of the overpass at Belorussian train station, Tverskaya becomes the main road out of the city, changing its name to **Leningradsky prospekt**. Just past the Dinamo soccer stadium is a miniature Kremlin, in red brick and white stone, with crenellated walls and towers. This is **Petrovsky Palace**, built in 1782 under Catherine the Great by the architect Kazakov as an overnight station for the imperial retinue on their way from St Petersburg to Moscow: a place to rest and dress for the ceremonial entrance into the city. In 1812, Napoleon left the burning city and stayed here. In Soviet times it was the Zhukovsky Air Force Academy. Today it serves as a reception site for the Moscow city government.

The city of Moscow ends and Moscow *oblast* (province) begins at the Outer Ring Road. At the turn-off to Sheremetyevo

Airport, overshadowed by an enormous shopping mall, stands the **Monument to the Defenders of Moscow** (Памятник защитникам Москвы, Pamyatnik zashchitnikam Moskvy). Three giant tank traps mark the spot where the German Army was stopped in its advance on the capital.

ULITSA VOLKHONKA & THE SOUTHWEST

The area to the southwest of the Kremlin has the highest concentration of art in the city, with four major museums and the magnificent state cathedral all on one short street, Volkhonka. Beyond Volkhonka is a former aristocratic neighbourhood that leads to the New Maiden Convent and cemetery, and then over the river to the Sparrow Hills and one of the best views of the city.

ART ROW

Ulitsa Volkhonka starts at Borovitskaya ploshchad. The **State Pushkin Museum of Fine Arts ®** (Государственный музей изобразительных искусств им. А.С.Пушкина, Gosudarstvenny muzey izobrazitelnykh iskusstv im. A.S. Pushkina; Volkhonka 12; Tue–Sun 10am–7pm; English audio players and museum maps available in the basement) is housed in a handsome

NON-CONFORMIST ART

During most of the Soviet period, 'non-conformist' art (anything that was non-representational and did not conform to official canons) was banned from public exhibition, and non-conformist artists were persecuted, jailed, incarcerated in psychiatric hospitals, or exiled. During the 1960s–80s, this underground art was largely sold to Western collectors. In the waning years of the USSR, attention was turned to the Soviet 'unofficial' artistic heritage, but much of the best works had already left the country.

Pushkin Museum

classical building that was founded as a museum by Ivan Tsvetaev, father of the poet Marina Tsvetaeva, to show Western art to the masses. The museum was opened in 1912 and after the Revolution it was enlarged by expropriated art collections and by 'trophy art' acquired during World War II. The greatest treasure removed from Germany during the war was the Schliemann Gold from ancient Troy. Only in 1993 did the museum authorities admit it was in their possession.

Today the museum has more than half a million works representing every period in Ancient and Western art, and many halls with copies of antique and European statuary. It has fine collections of 17th-century Dutch art (including many canvases by Rembrandt) and Italian art of the 17th and 18th centuries. The extraordinary collection of French art, impressionists and post-impressionists, is now displayed in the Annex, to the left of the main building. Most of these works are from pre-Revolutionary private collections and include Renoir, Monet, Pissarro, Degas, Cézanne, Gauguin, Van Gogh, Bonnard and Vuillard, as well as many works by Picasso and Matisse.

Across a narrow lane is the **Museum of Private Collections** (Музей Личных Коллекций, Muzey Lichnykh Kollektsiy; Volkhonka 8/10; www.artprivatecollections.ru; Wed, Fri–Sun noon–8pm, Thu noon–9pm; main collection closed at the time of writing, but temporary exhibitions were open). Several important private collections are displayed in a beautifully curated space. They are highly idiosyncratic, ranging from folk art and icons to the best of Russia's avant-garde artists, Alexander Rodchenko and Varvara Stepanova.

Nearby is the **Nikolai Roerich International Centre Museum** (Международный Центр-Музей им. Н.К.Рериха, Mezhdunarodny Tsentr-Muzey imeni NK Rerikha, Maly Znamensky pereulok 3/5; Tue–Sun 11am–7pm), which displays works of this unusual artist, from set designs for Diaghilev ballets to ethereal scenes of the Himalayas where he spent much of his later life.

For a very different kind of art museum, take a look inside the unmistakable bright turquoise **Ilya Glazunov Museum** (Государственная картинная галерея Ильи Глазунова,

CULTURAL HOUSE-MUSEUMS

Moscow has many wonderful 'house-museums' and 'apartment museums', which offer a marvellous glimpse into daily life in past centuries.

The **House Museum of Tolstoy** (Музей-усадьба ЛН Толстого – Muzey-usadba LN Tolstovo, Ulitsa Lva Tolstovo 21) is the perfectly preserved house where Tolstoy and his large family spent 19 winters.

The tidy little pink **House of Anton Chekhov** (Дом-музей АП Чехова – Dom-muzey AP Chekhova, Sadovaya-Kudrinskaya ulitsa 6) is where the writer lived with his family from 1886–90.

The **Maxim Gorky Museum**.

The **Pushkin Apartment Museum** (Мемориальный музей А.С. Пушкина – Memorialnaya kvartira AS Pushkina na Arbate; Ulitsa Arbat 53) was home to Pushkin and his bride Natalia just after they were married.

The **Skriabin House-Museum** (Мемориальный музей А.Н. Скриабина – Memorialny muzey AN Skriabina, Bolshoy Nikolopeskovsky pereulok 11) has preserved the composer's possessions.

Cathedral of Christ the Saviour

Gosudarstvennaya kartin-naya galereya Ili Glazunova; Volkhonka 13; www.glazunov.ru; Tue–Wed, Fri–Sun 11am–7pm, Thu 11am–9pm), which displays the canvases of this contemporary painter – considered nationalistic by many – as well as his icon collection.

CATHEDRAL OF CHRIST THE SAVIOUR

The **Cathedral of Christ the Saviour ⑲** (Храм Христа Спасителя, Khram Khrista Spasitelya; Volkhonka 15; daily 10am–5pm; free), sometimes translated as Christ the Redeemer, was built between 1839 and 1883 to commemorate Russia's victory over Napoleon in 1812. Destroyed by Stalin in 1931, it was rebuilt immediately after the 'second Russian revolution' and consecrated on 31 December 1999. In 2007 the body of President Yeltsin, who had instigated the rebuilding, lay in state here. This is Russia's largest church: over 103m (338ft) high and large enough to hold 10,000 worshippers. The cupola is gilded with 53kg (117lb) of a titanium and gold alloy, and is nearly 30m (98ft) in diameter. On the lower floor are kiosks and a small museum of the history of the church in Russia and the cathedral, which includes fragments of the original frescoes that were saved, as well as a remarkable collection of icons and holy relics. In 2012, the Russian female punk band, Pussy Riot, staged an anti-Putin protest at the cathedral. The band members' subsequent trial and imprisonment caused international outrage and they were released by President Putin before Russia hosted the Winter Olympics in 2014.

The nearby streets of Ostozhenka and Prechistinka were once home to the aristocracy, and it is pleasant to stroll along these little lanes, admiring the old manor houses and renovated apartment buildings. The **Academy of the Arts** (Prechistenka 21), built 1788–93, is considered one of Moscow's finest examples of classicism. Restored in 2000, it houses an art gallery. Next door, at No. 19, is one of many Zurab Tsereteli galleries.

Just beyond the Garden Ring Road near the Park Kultury metro station is the **Church of St Nikolay the Wonderworker in Khamovniki**. Built in the late 17th century by weavers (khamovniki), its bright green and orange-red domes make it one of Moscow's most striking churches.

Nearby, is the **Museum of Moscow** (Музей Москвы, Muzey Moskvy; Zubovsky bulvar 2; www.mosmuseum.ru; Tue, Wed, Fri–Sun 10am–8pm, Thu 11am–9pm, closed last Fri of the month). The museum's extensive collection includes reconstructions of daily life in medieval Moscow and a scale model of the Kremlin surrounded by water on all three sides.

NEW MAIDEN CONVENT

Not far from Khamovniki stands **New Maiden Convent and Cemetery ⑳**. New Maiden Convent is one of the best preserved and most peaceful of Moscow's fortress cloisters (Новодевичий монастырь, Novodevichy monastyr; Novodevichy proezd 1; Wed–Mon 9am–5pm, closed first Mon of the month).

Oh, brother

Peter the Great sent his sister, Sophia, to the convent after her second attempt to gain the throne. She tried to organise a mutiny of the streltsy (musketeers) in 1698. Peter put down the mutiny and had several of the streltsy hanged under Sophia's convent window.

The convent was founded in 1524, and for most of its history it was a kind of prison for unwanted royal women, including Irina Godunova, Tsar Fyodor's widow and the sister of Boris Godunov, and Sophia, Peter the Great's scheming older sister. As a result it was richly endowed, and the convent built churches second only to the Kremlin in size and magnificence. Made a museum in 1922, it was partially returned to the church in 1944.

Beside the river and a popular small lake, this peaceful corner of bustling Moscow is guarded by tall brick walls similar to the Kremlin battlements. The central church is the **Smolensk Cathedral** (Смоленский собор, Smolensky Sobor), built in 1525 with a magnificent five-tiered iconostasis (1683–85) and richly decorated walls and frescoes. Tombs of nuns, military leaders and wealthy families are scattered about the grounds, including the beautiful family crypt of the Prokhorov textile magnates in front of the cathedral, which was built in 1911 in the *style moderne*.

The museum found in the **Lopukhin Chambers** displays a variety of temporary exhibits. A permanent exhibition of ecclesiastical vestments and vessels, icons and frescoes is displayed in the **Irina Godunova Chambers**.

The tranquil Novodevichy, or New Maiden Convent

NEW MAIDEN CEMETERY

A separate cemetery opened beside the convent in 1904 and immediately became the most prestigious in the city. The Soviet government continued the tradition, interring military, artistic and political leaders. **New Maiden Cemetery** (Новодевичье

Moscow State University on the Sparrow Hills

кладбище, Novodeviche kladbishche, Luzhnetsky proezd 2; daily 9am–5pm; free) is a who's who of Russia's prominent citizens including Chekhov, Gogol, Mayakovsky, Shostakovich, Raisa Gorbachev, Boris Yeltsin and Mstislav Rostropovich. Perhaps the most striking grave is Nikita Khrushchev's, by sculptor Ernst Neizvestny. His bust rests between white and black blocks, symbolising his positive and negative legacies.

THE SPARROW HILLS

On top of a high bluff across the Moscow River from New Maiden Convent are the **Sparrow Hills** (Воробьевы горы, Vorobyovy gory), once a favourite spot for Muscovites to rent dachas in the hot summer months and enjoy the fabulous view over the city. Anton Chekhov once said, 'If you want to understand Russia, you must come here and look out over Moscow'. It's still a magnificent view, enjoyed by newlywed couples who come to the site to be photographed. Behind the viewing platform is the main building of the **Moscow State University**, greatest of the Stalin

Pond life

The neighbourhood to the northwest of Nikitsky Gates is one of the city's most elite residential areas, with many upscale shops and cafés, particularly lining the Patriarch's Ponds.

skyscrapers. The university has more than 50 buildings with 6,000 student rooms, spread about an enormous park and botanical gardens. In evenings in spring, the air is still filled with the songs of nightingales.

FROM THE ARBAT TO THE WEST

The area to the west of the Kremlin has several distinct neighbourhoods that are pleasant for strolling. The Old and New Arbat streets have changed over the centuries, but still are traditional shopping districts. Beyond the Garden Ring Road is the Krasnaya Presnya district, the venue of bloody street fighting in both of the 20th-century's Russian revolutions. On the far side of the river are monuments to the two 'patriotic wars' – 1812 and World War II.

ARBAT SQUARE AND ENVIRONS

Ulitsa Vozdvizhenka used to be lined with a row of princely mansions. One of the few that remains is at No. 16: a Moorish-style palace built in 1899 by the magnate Arseny Morozov. During the Soviet period, it was the House of Friendship and it is now a state reception venue. It stands in stark contrast to the white marble box of the **State Lenin Library**. Built in 1940, and known colloquially as 'Leninka', this is the main library in the country and houses more than 40 million volumes. A large statue of Dostoyevsky, who spent many hours in the library, stands outside.

Just past the Lenin Library, the **Shchusev Museum of Architecture** (Музей архитектуры им. А.В. Щусева, Muzey arkhitektury im. AV Shchuseva; Ulitsa Vozdvizhenka 5/25; www.

muar.ru; Tue–Wed, Fri–Sun 10am–8pm, Thu 1–9pm) holds temporary exhibitions while being restored and developed.

Ulitsa Vozdvizhenka meets the Boulevard Ring at **Arbat Square** (Площадь Арбатские Ворота, Arbetskaya vorota ploshchad), a White City gate and now a mass of kiosks and commercial mayhem. But the boulevard to the right (with one's back to the Kremlin) is a pleasant strolling street, with leafy trees and park benches in the centre and plenty of cafés along the way. Stop at the **Museum of Oriental Art ㉑** (Государственный музей Востока, Gosudarstvenny muzey Vostoka; Nikitsky bulvar 12a; www.orientmuseum.ru; Tue, Fri–Sun 11am–8pm, Wed–Thu noon–9pm) to see a small, high-quality collection of Eastern art, with rare rugs from the Middle East and Caucasus.

'The Wave' staircase in the Maxim Gorky Museum

The Boulevard Ring meets Bolshaya Nikitskaya ulitsa at **Nikitsky Gates** (Никитские ворота, Nikitskie vorota), another former White City entry gate. On one corner is the modern ITAR-TASS building, on the other the majestic **Church of the Great Ascension**, where the country's greatest poet, Alexander Pushkin, married the country's greatest beauty, Natalya Goncharova, in 1831. They were married only a few years before Pushkin was killed in a duel with a Frenchman who

Crowds on Old Arbat Street

had been pressing his favours on the beautiful Natalya.

Just off the square at the corner of Ulitsa Spiridonovka and Malaya Nikitskaya is one of Moscow's most brilliant *style moderne* mansions. Built by Fyodor Shekhtel in 1900 for the banker Ryabushinsky, it is now the **Maxim Gorky Museum** ㉒ (Музей-квартира А.М. Горького, Muzey-kvartira AM Gorkovo; Malaya Nikitskaya 6/2; Wed–Sun 11am–5.30pm, closed last Thu of the month; free; room descriptions in English). The writer lived here from 1931 to his death under house arrest in 1936. The interior of swirling ornamentation, including the magnificent curved limestone staircase called 'The Wave', has been meticulously restored.

OLD AND NEW ARBAT

The labyrinth of lanes in a vast area stretching between Prechistinka and Povarskaya ulitsas are still called the 'Arbat lanes' in reference to **Old Arbat Street** ㉓ (Арбат). The name is believed to come from the Turkic word *rabat*, meaning 'caravan', and was first settled by traders from the south. By the end of the 1900s, the area was home to Moscow's poets, writers and artists. Today the **Old Arbat** is a lively pedestrian street day or night: filled with cafés, souvenir and antique shops, with portrait artists, photographers, singers, dancers and fun-seekers.

There are several interesting sights and literary museums (see page 55) on and around the Arbat. Just off the Arbat at Krivoarbatsky pereulok 10 is the Constructivist masterpiece of the **Melnikov House**. Designed by Konstantin Melnikov in 1929, it was the only private residence built during the Soviet period. It has been the subject of a bitter inheritance dispute in recent years, and is not open to the public.

On the other side of the Arbat, Spasopeskovsky pereulok leads to the charming white stone **Church of the Transfiguration of the Saviour on the Sands**. The five-domed church was built in 1689 with a lovely tent spire over the belfry.

Nearby is Spaso House, a beautiful neo-classical mansion built in 1913; it has been the American ambassador's residence since 1933.

New Arbat (Новый Арбат, Novy Arbat), which is to the north of Old Arbat, was an elite address when it was laid out in the 1960s. Today it is an uninspired mix of shopping malls, nightclubs and drab block buildings, and a night-time haunt. Only the pretty white 17th-century **Church of Simeon the Stylite** was saved from the wrecker's ball.

KUDRINSKAYA SQUARE AND THE GARDEN RING ROAD

The boundary of the 'Arbat lanes', Povarskaya ulitsa, ends at **Kudrinskaya Square** (Кудринская площадь, Kudrinskaya ploshchad), part of the Garden Ring Road with one of the Stalinist 'birthday cake' buildings. Completed in 1954, it houses apartments and a weather observatory under its spire.

Nearby is the **Fyodor Chalyapin Museum** (Дом-музей Ф.И. Шаляпина, Dom-muzey FI Shalyapina, Novinsky bulvar 25; Tue, Sat 10am–6pm, Wed–Thu 11.30am–7pm, Sun 10am–4.30pm, closed last day of the month; concerts and other events). The lush house that this famous singer (1873–1938) lived in is filled with memorabilia.

BEYOND THE RING ROAD

'The Tragedy of Nations', Victory Park

The Krasnaya Presnya neighbourhood was the site of street battles in 1905 and 1917, and again in the 1990s near the **White House**, then the Council of Ministers building. During the coup attempt in 1991, it was the rallying point for Yeltsin's supporters; in 1993, the building was occupied by the parliament opposed to Yeltsin and fired upon until the opposition leaders surrendered. By the White House there is a small monument to those who died in the events of 1991 and 1993 and the historic **Hunchbacked Bridge**, built in 1683 when it crossed the narrow Presnya River, now underground. The bridge figured prominently in the 1905 fighting.

For a sense of the various Russian revolutions, visit the **Museum of Krasnaya Presnya** (Музей Красная Пресня, Muzey Krasnaya Presnya; Bolshoy Predtechensky pereulok 4; Tue–Wed, Fri–Sun 11am–7pm, Thu noon–9pm, closed last Fri of the month). The museum displays a history of the revolutionary movements and has a room-sized diorama of the 1905 battles, with sound effects.

KUTUZOVSKY PROSPEKT AND VICTORY PARK

As Novy Arbat crosses the Moscow River, it becomes **Kutuzovsky prospekt**, where, from the 1950s, Soviet leaders lived in enormous apartments. The 12-lane highway is clogged with traffic to the elite dacha communities to the west of the city and not a fun place for strolling. But there are several important historical museums here.

The **Battle of Borodino Panorama Museum** (Музей-панорама Бородинская битва, Muzey-panorama Borodinskaya bitva; Kutuzovsky prospekt 38; www.1812panorama.ru; Sat–Wed 10am–6pm, Thu 10am–9pm, closed last Thu of the month) has a 115-m (492-ft) circular painting depicting the key battle outside Moscow in 1812. It was painted by Franz Rubo in 1912 and installed in this specially constructed, circular building in 1962.

Just past the **Triumphal Arch**, which was designed by Osip Bovet and stood on the square in front of Belorussian train station from 1829 to 1936, is the great expanse of **Victory Park ㉔**.

In the centre of the park, amid lovely fountains, is a 140-m/ 460-ft obelisk decorated by Zurab Tsereteli with the angel of victory and a sculpture of bronze figures called '**The Tragedy**

ZURAB THE GREAT

Visitors to Moscow would be forgiven for thinking that there is just one sculptor in the entire city: Zurab Tsereteli. He is President of the Russian Academy of Arts, has several museums based on his work and private collections, and is the creator of more than a dozen high-profile monuments in Moscow. Muscovites like some of them (the entrance to the zoo and Manège Square) and dislike others (Peter the Great). Some people, like former mayor Yuri Luzhkov, think he's a genius. Still others, like the 10,000 people who signed an internet petition protesting against the artist's plans to do a sculpture of poet and Nobel Prize-winner Joseph Brodsky, think he's the king of kitsch. Zurab Tsereteli doesn't seem to care what anyone thinks, and enjoys his fame and wealth with enviable pleasure. However history will judge his works, there is no question that he has left his mark on Moscow, from the monument in Victory Park to the statue of Charles de Gaulle in front of the Kosmos Hotel.

of Nations'. Around the monument a church, mosque and synagogue have been built for religious observances. The main attraction of the park is **Central Museum of the Great Patriotic War** (Парк Победы, Park Pobedy, and Центральный музей Великой Отечественной Войны, Tsentralny muzey Velikoy Otechestvennoy Voiny; Tue–Wed, Sat–Sun 10am–8pm, Thu–Fri 10am–8.30pm; entry to park is free), which displays the progress of World War II in detail.

Despite the subject of the park, it has become one of Moscow's liveliest fair-weather outdoor venues, and is packed with rollerbladers, flirting teens, kids climbing the tanks – and grandmothers keeping an eye on both.

Lovers of architecture should not miss the nearby **Church of the Intercession at Fili ㉕** (Церковь Покрова в Филях, Tserkov Pokrova v Filyakh; Ulitsa Novozavodskaya 6; daily 8am–6pm). This 17th-century baroque church is a pale, frothy wedding cake crowned by six golden domes. In the upper (summer) church one entire wall is covered with a nine-tiered iconostasis with dozens of icons framed in heavily ornamented and gilded carved wood. During services, the Naryshkin family that built the church and their royal guests used to sit in the gilded Tsar's Box opposite.

LUBYANKA SQUARE AND THE NORTH

Before the 1917 Revolution **Lubyanka Square** (Лубянская площадь, Lubyanskaya ploshchad) was a busy market area where carters and carriage drivers stabled their horses and rested in cheap taverns. But all that changed when the Bolsheviks expropriated the Russia Insurance Company building for the secret police

Zoo stop

For a break from traffic and museums, spend a few hours in the Moscow Zoo (Bolshaya Gruzinskaya ulitsa 1; Tue–Sun 10am–8pm).

(formerly KGB, now FSB) and began to build other buildings around – and even underneath – this notorious square.

Although most of the major buildings on the square still belong to the FSB, the neighbourhood is a busy commercial district, with several interesting museums and sights. A few have associations with the square's past: the **Detsky Mir** (Children's World) store was built opposite the KGB headquarters in 1957, supposedly due to the concern over orphans by the KGB founder Felix Dzerzhinsky. At the end of the square by the Russian Revival-style Polytechnic Museum is the **Monument to the Victims of the Totalitarian Regime** (Памятник жертвам тоталитарного режима, Pamyatnik zhertvam totalitarnovo rezhima). This simple stone is from the island monastery that became Solovki prison camp in Russia's Far North.

Moscow's famous sights are given a Lego workover at Central Children's Store

The **Polytechnic Museum** (Политехнический музей, Politekhnichesky muzey; www.polymus.ru; Tue–Sun 10am–8pm, closed last Fri of the month) was built in 1907 and has a huge collection of gadgets and devices, from ancient timepieces to space equipment.

On the north side of the square is a bust of the futurist poet Vladimir Mayakovsky, which marks the site of the **Mayakovsky Museum** 26 (Музей В.В. Маяковского, Muzey VV Mayakovskovo;

Perlov Tea Shop

Fri–Tue 11am–7pm, Thu 1–9pm, closed last Fri of the month). The museum, which is entered through an archway, has preserved the modest room where Mayakovsky lived and committed suicide in 1930. The rest of the museum is a swirl of futurist manifestos, hand-drawn posters, constructivist drawings and models, manuscripts, letters, posters and photographs of his plays.

AROUND LUBYANKA SQUARE

Nearby Myasnitskaya ulitsa (Butcher's Street) is the typical post-Soviet Moscow mish-mash of shops, bars and cafés. Noteworthy at the far end is the *faux* Chinese **Perlov Tea Shop**, built in 1890 by a tea merchant to impress the Chinese Emperor on his state visit.

On Bolshaya Lubyanka, another street that spokes off from Lubyanka Square, is the **Sretensky Monastery**. Founded in 1397 and restored to the church in 1994, it includes the **Church of the Icon of the Vladimir Mother of God**, nestled behind the monastery's lovely white stone wall. In any season the intimate cloister is a welcome haven.

Small **Kuznetsky Most**, one of the city's best-known shopping streets, was originally the 'Smithy's Bridge' that crossed the Neglinnaya River. When the river went underground it was taken apart and used to make Moscow's most aristocratic shopping street. In the 19th century it was filled with tiny French fashion and jewellery shops. Today there are *haute couture* boutiques, a jewellery store called Fabergé, an English language bookstore (No. 18/7), an exhibition space (No. 15) in the Moscow Union of Artists, and a hippie health-food store and vegetarian café, Jagannath (No. 11).

BOULEVARDS UPON BOULEVARDS

Neglinnaya ulitsa, which follows the path of the underground river, is perhaps best known for the **Sandunovsky Bath House** (Neglinnaya ulitsa 14, str. 3–7; tel: 495-782 1808; www.sanduny.ru). The men's side is sumptuously decorated; the women's side less so, but both sides are a treat for weary travellers (see page 90).

At nearby **Trubnaya Square** (Трубная площадь, Trubnaya ploshchad) four boulevards come together. Tsvetnoy leads north, Petrovsky to Pushkin Square in the west, and Rozhdestvensky leads up a steep hill to the east. As the boulevard rises, the central park grows wider until it is a vast expanse with a pond at **Chistye Prudy** (Clean Ponds), enjoyed by swans and skaters. Chistye Prudy is another of Moscow's expensive residential and commercial neighbourhoods.

TWO ARTISTIC BROTHERS

Just northeast of the Chistye Prudy area is a house-museum of a brilliant artist. The small **Apollary Vasnetsov Museum** (Музей-квартира А.М. Васнецова, Muzey-kvartira AM Vasnetsova; Furmanny pereulok 6, apt 21-22, press '22' on the house phone and go up to the third floor;

Diamonds

The Russian region of Yakutia (now called Sakha) produces more diamonds than anywhere else in the world. These bright, clear jewels have been faceted at a shop in Smolensk for decades. Buy them at Smolenskie Brillianty, Kuznetsky Most 18/7.

Friendship of Nations fountain

www.tretyakovgallery.ru; Wed–Sun 10am–5pm) is filled with wonderful paintings and drawings of old Moscow in the era before Peter the Great.

Apollary's brother Viktor is famous for his set designs and enormous canvases of Russian fairy and folk tales. Across the ring road, east of Mira prospekt, is the **Viktor Vasnetsov House-Museum** 27 (Дом-музей В.М. Васнецова, Dom-muzey VM Vasnetsova, Pereulok Vasnetsova 13; www.tretyakovgallery. ru; Wed–Sun 10am–5pm; closed last Thu of the month), hidden in the middle of a depressing housing estate. Vasnetsov built the house – half Russian hut, half fairy tale cottage – in 1894 and lived here until his death in 1926. The interior is filled with *style moderne* and folk furniture and crafts.

BEYOND THE RING ROAD

Scattered about the city to the north of the Garden Ring Road are a number of interesting sites. Near Novoslobodskaya metro is the **Museum of Decorative and Applied Art and Folk Art**

(Музей декоративно-прикладного и народного искусства, Muzey dekorativno-prikladnovo i narodnovo iskusstva; Delegatskaya ulitsa 3; Mon, Wed–Fri, Sun 10am–6pm, Sat noon–8pm, closed last Mon of the month), which has an enormous collection of crafts, folk costumes and applied arts. Nearby is the **Museum of the Armed Forces** (Музей Вооружённых сил, Muzey Vooruzhyonnykh sil, Ulitsa Sovietskoy armii 2; Wed–Fri and Sun 10am–5pm, Sat 11am–7pm). It displays the history of the armed forces from the 18th century to the present. It is across the street from the **Soviet Army Theatre**, in the shape of a five-pointed star. In the vicinity, near Maryina Roshcha metro is the **Jewish Museum and Tolerance Center** (Еврейский музей и центр толерантности, Yevreysky muzey i tsentr tolerantnosti, Ulitsa Obraztsova 11, str. 1A; www.jewish-museum.ru; Sun–Thu noon–10pm, Fri 10am–3pm), a very engaging and modern museum, which is thought to be the largest Jewish museum in the world. It was opened in 2012 in the restored Bakhmetevsky Bus Garage.

AROUND VDNKH METRO STATION

The metro station here bears the name of the **Exhibition of Achievements of National Economy** ㉘ (Выставка достижений народного хозяйства, Vystavka Dostizheniy Narodnovo Khozaystva [VDNKh]; www.vdnh.ru; park 24/7, free, most sites daily 10am–11pm). The VDNKh, which opened in 1939, is an odd hybrid; with more than 400 buildings spread over 2.4 sq. km (1 sq. mile). It has the most spectacular Soviet-realist architecture, with shops selling items from puppies to washing machines – with some crafts and souvenirs as well. There are two magnificent fountains: the **Friendship of Nations fountain**, with

Mayor's line

Local residents call the elevated railway near the VDNKh metro station 'Mayor Luzhkov's Folly' because of the enormous cost of such a short line.

Memorial Museum of Cosmonautics

golden collective-farm maidens representing the Soviet republics dancing under 800 jets of water, and the fairy tale **Stone Flower fountain**. Around this main square are some of the best-preserved pavilions. Pavilion 71 (directly north of the towered building) has a small and quirky **Ice Age Museum-Theatre** (Музей-театр ледниковый период, Muzey-teatr lednikovy period; closed for restoration), which has skeletons, reconstructed woolly mammoths and a furry rhinoceros.

The Circular Cinema there has another Soviet oddity: films-in-the-round. The 20-minute films (Fri, Sat and Sun at noon, 1pm, 2.30pm, 4pm, 5pm, 6pm and 7pm when there are at least four visitors), shot on synchronised cameras to form a 360-degree view, were made in the 1960s and 1970s and show the USSR that even old-timers have forgotten.

The VDNKh also is also home to the open-air Green Theatre, which reopened in 2014 after meticulous restoration, and a complex of four pools inaugurated in 2015.

A few blocks from the entry to the exhibition grounds towers Vera Mukhina's iconic **Monument to the Worker and Collective Farm Woman** (Prospekt Mira 123b, exhibition rooms Tue–Sun noon–9pm). The restored monument, originally created for the 1937 World's Fair in Paris, towers 24.5m (78ft) into the sky, on a pedestal of 34.5m (113ft).

By the VDNKh metro is the one-room **Memorial Museum of Cosmonautics** (Музей Космонавтики, Muzey Kosmonavtiki, Prospekt Mira 111; Tue, Wed, Fri, Sun 10am–7pm, Thu, Sat 10am–9pm, closed last Fri of the month) in the base of the space rocket soaring nearly 100m (330 ft) above the city. The largest part of the exhibition is devoted to Yuri Gagarin's first space flight in April 1961, but there are sections devoted to every other Russian space programme, manned and otherwise, including canine flights. The first dogs to make a round trip into space, Belka and Strelka, have been stuffed for posterity and are on display.

OSTANKINO ESTATE

Not far from the metro station is the **Ostankino Estate Museum** ㉙ (Музей-усадьба Останкино, Muzey-usadba Ostankino; Ulitsa 1-aya Ostankinskaya 5; www.ostankino-museum. ru; long-term renovation began in 2013, some items from the collection will be shown at exhibitions; check website for more details). The estate was built by Count Nikolay Sheremetev in 1797 as a theatre-palace: an entire estate as a kind of stage for evenings of music, light shows, feasts and entertainment. Many of the magnificent rooms in the Italian Pavilion are being restored, but the rooms and halls open to visitors are sumptuous, with spacious meeting rooms and niches where guests could chat. The Ostankino 'theatre within a theatre' is the only remaining 18th-century palace-theatre in Russia. Cleverly designed with columns that could be shifted around the stage (and machines that made the sound of rain and wind), the entire seating area could be covered instantly by flooring to serve as a banquet hall after the festivities. During the summer months Ostankino holds early music concerts in the theatre. Be sure to leave time to wander through the romantically landscaped park. The dark red-brick **Church of**

the **Life-Giving Trinity** on the grounds was built 1678–92.

SOUTH OF THE RIVER

The area south of the river is called Zamoskvoreche – 'Beyond the Moscow River'. This low-lying area was flood-prone and still not incorporated in the city proper in the 19th century when the cheap land was purchased for factories. Industrialists built a great number of churches that still grace the narrow streets. Today there are two main areas of interest to visitors.

Monument to Peter the Great on the Moskva River

BOG ISLAND

To halt the constant flooding, in 1783 a **Drainage Canal** (Vodootvodny Kanal) was cut, forming a long island between the canal and the Moscow River. **Bog Island** (Болотный остров, Bolotny Ostrov) had a main square, **Bog Square** beside which is the **House on the Embankment** (Дом на Набережной, Dom na Naberezhnoy) commissioned in the late 1920s for high Communist Party officials. More than 100 ministers and 150 deputy ministers lived here, including Khrushchev and Stalin's daughter, Svetlana Alliluyeva. During the Stalinist purges over 700 officials and their families were arrested, executed or exiled from the house. A sculptural group, **'Children Are the Victims of Adults' Vices'**, by Mikhail Shemyakin, can be seen here.

At the tip of the island, accessible by bridges from the Christ the Saviour Church and the Krymskaya naberezhnaya, stands Zurab Tsereteli's most controversial statue: the enormous monument to the **300th Anniversary of the Russian Navy**, with Peter the Great towering on three ships over the narrow stretch of river. The former Red October Chocolate Factory adjacent to it is now home to several galleries of contemporary art and photography, avant-garde shops, cafés and bars.

THE TRETYAKOV GALLERY

Near the river is the **Tretyakov Gallery** ❸⓿ (Государственная Третьяковская галерея, Gosudarstvennaya Tretyakovskaya galereya; Lavrushinsky pereulok 12; Tue, Wed, Sun 10am–6pm, Thu, Fri, Sat 10am–9pm; Church of St Nicholas in Tolmachi; www.tretyakovgallery.ru; Tue–Sun noon–4pm; free English room map at information desk), which holds the world's largest collection of Russian art.

Pavel Tretyakov (1832–98) bought his first paintings in 1856 and continued to amass a spectacular collection for the next three decades. He opened his collection to the public in 1881 and left it to the city in his will. The old Russian style façade was designed for the house in 1904 by Viktor Vasnetsov (see page 70).

The museum consists of more than 130,000 works of art covering the most ancient Russian art up to the avant-garde period (art from the beginning of the 20th century to the present is housed in the New Tretyakov Gallery, see page 77). In 1997 the

The Wanderers

Ilya Repin (1844–1930) is Russia's best known artist. A realist, he painted local subjects out of doors and was one of a group of painters known as The Wanderers. One of his finest paintings in the Tretyakov Gallery captures the moment after Ivan the Terrible struck and killed his son (Hall 29).

Church of St Nicholas in Tolmachi was renovated to house art and is now connected through underground passages to the museum. In this church-museum, rare icons are venerated by the pious but protected by modern technology.

The Tretyakov collection is designed to be seen chronologically starting on the first floor with early 18th-century works, which mark the beginning of secular art in Russia. The halls take visitors through the decades, from academy painting in the first halls through the canvases of the Wanderers, who depicted Russian life in all its variety – and are as fascinating historically as they are artistically. The period of famous 'isms' – expressionism, symbolism and impressionism – leading up to the great explosion in avant-garde art is also well represented.

The ground floor halls display an amazing collection of religious art. Be sure to see the extraordinary icons by Andrey Rublyov (1360/70–1430s). The *Old Testament Trinity* was taken from the Trinity Cathedral in the Holy Trinity Monastery of St Sergius (see page 82). Even without an eye attuned to the canons of iconography, Rublyov's works are easily distinguishable by their luminous, emotional quality, one that has not been achieved by any other icon painter.

The museum also has a small **Treasury** (Hall 55) that displays precious ecclesiastical and secular objects in a dimly lit and climate-controlled environment.

AROUND THE GALLERY

Also on Lavrushinsky pereulok, is the Tretyakov Gallery's **Engineering Building** (Инженерный корпус; Lavrushinsky pereulok 12; www.tretyakovgallery.ru; Tue, Wed, Sun 10am–6pm, Thu, Fri, Sat 10am–9pm) which holds temporary exhibitions. The **Church of St Nicholas at Tolmachi museum** contains a collection of icons, including the national palladium, the 12th-century icon of 'The Virgin of Vladimir'.

The main streets near the museum, **Bolshaya Ordynka** and **Pyatnitskaya**, and small side streets in between have not been totally ruined by the building boom and have many pleasures, notably a plethora of churches built by merchants' and artisans' guilds. Pyatnitskaya ulitsa is fronted by small pastel-coloured buildings filled with shops and cafés.

Fun fair in Gorky Park

GORKY PARK

The other area for art-lovers 'beyond the river' is Krymsky Val, across the bridge from the Park Kultury metro station. **Gorky Park** (www.park-gorkogo.com; open all day, free), established in 1928 as a fairground, is best known to English-speakers from the 1980s detective novel *Gorky Park* by Martin Cruz Smith in which three young women ice skaters are murdered here. Murder and mayhem rarely occur in this pleasure park, but skating remains popular when its paths are flooded and frozen in the winter. The park still has some fine examples of socialist realist architecture and is a calm oasis of nature on the banks of the river.

NEW TRETYAKOV GALLERY

The **New Tretyakov Gallery** ❸ (Государственная Третья-ковская галерея на Крымском Валу, Gosudarstvennaya Tretyakovskaya galereya na Krymskom Valu; Krymsky Val

10/14; www.tretyakovgallery.ru; Tue, Wed, Sun 10am–6pm, Thu, Fri, Sat 10am–9pm) on Krymsky Val houses the museum's collection of art of the 20th century.

The highlight is the spectacular avant-garde from the turn of the 20th century, when Kazimir Malevich, Vasiy Kandinsky, Vladimir Tatlin, Lyubov Popova and Alexander Rodchenko revolutionised art. Soon after the Revolution, the avant-garde fell out of favour, but the collection has a surprisingly full range of styles from the Soviet period – even though many canvases were hidden under the bed until the 1980s.

Behind the building (accessed from the embankment) is the **Muzeon Sculpture Park** (daily 8am–11pm in spring and summer and 8am–10pm in autumn and winter). It started life in the 1991 coup attempt, when Soviet monuments were pulled down and dumped here. Some years later, the authorities opened a park with more than 600 sculptures of all trends and schools. Soviet monuments in this 'park of fallen idols' are on pedestals once again.

House of Artists

Confusingly, the entrance along the 'short' side of the building opposite Gorky Park leads to an entirely different organisation, the Central House of Artists, which has a large exhibition space for art, antique and other art-related fairs. Small galleries and shops here sell art books, jewellery, applied arts and crafts.

FURTHER AFIELD

Every Friday afternoon Muscovites flood the highways out of the city in the Great Dacha Exodus. If you want to see a bit of rural Russia, join the traffic and head out to an ancient monastery town or a country estate. Some palaces that were once outside the city proper are now accessible by metro.

Palace at Kolomenskoe

KOLOMENSKOE

Dating from the 14th century, **Kolomenskoe** ❸❷ (Коломенское; Andropova prospekt 39; www.mgomz.com; park compound, daily Apr–Oct 9am–10pm, Nov–Mar 9am–7pm, museums Tue–Sun 11am–7pm, park free) was one of the earliest summer palaces built outside the city for the grand princes and tsars. During the Soviet period, it was a showcase for wooden architecture and stone monuments from all over Russia. Today it offers a glimpse at almost every period in Russian history, along with cafés, a children's playground, an outdoor fair, and weekend folk festivals.

The most important church on the lovely grounds is the extraordinary **Church of the Ascension** (Церковь Вознесения Господня, Tserkov Vozneseniya Gospodnya), built in 1532. The church has a stone spire rising up 62m/203ft, with decorative rows of gables over the bays and galleries around the base.

The two museum buildings have excellent collections of wood carvings, crafts, tiles, ecclesiastical vestments and icons. The highlight of the museum is the exact model of Tsar Alexei's wooden palace folly, a crazy maze of buildings, *terems* and churches that has been reconstructed on another part of the grounds.

Among the wooden structures is the **rustic cabin** Peter the Great lived in while in the northern city of Arkhangelsk. Tsar Peter spent some of his childhood in Kolomenskoe.

KUSKOVO

Kuskovo (Кусково; Ulitsa Yunosti 2; Wed–Sun buildings and grotto 10am–6pm, park 10am–8pm, closed last Wed of the month) vies with several other estates around Moscow for the title of the 'Russian Versailles' and provides a time-travel trip back to the days of luxurious royal life. Built by the Sheremetev family in the late 18th century, it is one of the best preserved of Moscow's estate palaces with a lovely formal garden reflected in a serene pond. It also has a magnificent collection of ceramics and porcelain.

More than 20 buildings are set among the gardens and pond, including the **Dutch House**, the **Italian House**, the **Hermitage**, and the oldest building on the grounds, the family church (1739) which is virtually unchanged. Three of the buildings are open at present. In the **Palace**, visitors can see the ballroom, several sitting rooms and the bedroom, all decorated with silk wallpaper, rich parquet floors and lush frescoes. The **Grotto** was built in 1755–61 to look like a baroque underwater cave and is festooned with fragments of shells, glass and porcelain embedded in stucco. The ceramics and porcelain museum is in the **Orangerie**.

Dachas

Dacha comes from the Russian 'to give' and originally meant a plot of land given to someone for service to the empire. Since pre-Revolutionary times, it has meant a summer cottage not far from a city.

TSARITSYNO

Tsaritsyno (Царицыно; Ultisa Dolskaya 1; museums Wed–Sun 11am–6pm, Sat until 8pm, closed last Wed of the month) is the strangest of Moscow's urban estates, because no one ever lived here. In 1775 Catherine the Great liked the village and bought it. She ordered neo-Gothic palaces to be built, but when she came to approve the construction, she rejected them all. The estate remained an evocative ghostly ruin until Moscow's former mayor Luzhkov decided to rewrite history. He rebuilt the palaces and turned them into

Grand Palace, Tsaritsyno

extravagant museums, with more gold and inlaid parquet floors than Catherine's palace outside St Petersburg.

Several of the pavilions have also been restored and house temporary and permanent exhibitions. It is still pleasant to stroll about the ruins, over the brick and stone bridges covered with stars, crosses and other Gothic ornamentation, and into the woods and meadows.

SERGEEV POSAD

If you are interested in Russian religious architecture and small-town life, a day trip to **Sergeev Posad** ❸❸ (Сергеев Посад) is a must. There is nothing as stirring as the first sight of the gold and azure cupolas of the Holy Trinity Monastery of St Sergius rising up over the thick white walls. The squares and lanes around

The Holy Trinity Monastery of St Sergius

the monastery are lined with charming wooden houses and imbued with a decidedly un-Muscovite peace and calm. The **Holy Trinity Monastery of St Sergius** (Свято-Троицкая Сергеева Лавра, Svyato-Troitskaya Sergeeva Lavra; suburban train from Yaroslavsky Station; tours through Patriarshy Dom – see page 123) was founded by St Sergius (1314–92). He played a profound role in secular and religious life, defining the country's monastic tradition, and his diplomatic missions to the principalities helped ensure the 'gathering of the Rus' that led to the formation of the Russian state.

The monastery suffered greatly over the centuries: during Tatar raids in the 15th century, the Polish incursion of 1608–10, and finally during the early years of Soviet power, when its monks were arrested and riches plundered. It was partially reopened in 1946 as a religious order and finally returned to the church in 1988. Today there are about 300 monks, a divinity academy, a seminary and schools for choirmasters and icon-painters.

INSIDE THE MONASTERY

There are several magnificent churches within the monastery, and a great turquoise and white bell tower (built between 1740 and 1770) that rises up 88m (280ft) in five tiers and has 42 bells (compared to 21 in the Kremlin's bell tower), including the largest in Russia, weighing 75 tonnes.

The oldest church is the **Trinity Cathedral** (Троицкий собор, Troitsky sobor), built in 1425. The exterior is severe, but the interior has some extraordinary icons and frescoes. The monk and brilliant icon-painter Andrey Rublyov painted the *Old Testament Trinity* for this church. The original is in the Tretyakov Gallery.

The largest church is the magnificent **Cathedral of the Dormition** (Успенский собор, Uspensky sobor) built between 1559–85 to replicate the church of the same name in the Kremlin. Inside is an enormous five-tiered iconostasis with 76 icons; the icons and frescoes were painted long after the church was completed in 1684.

The **Museum** (Ризница, Riznitsa), which is still state-run, has an extraordinary collection of ecclesiastical vestments, vessels, gold and jewel-encrusted Bible covers, religious embroidery and imperial gifts. The monastery also has a museum where the teaching of icon painting is taught; it includes a rare Coptic icon and carved icons from the Russian north, as well as gifts brought from pilgrimages to the Holy Land.

IN THE TOWN

Sergeev Posad is also famous for its toys: legend has it that a local craftsman carved the first *matryoshka* doll. The square outside the monastery gates has an open-air craft market and is lined with shops and cafés. The small lanes around the monastery have some lovely (though dilapidated) wooden houses with windows decorated with elaborate carvings.

Lucky escape

In 1682 Peter the Great and his brother were taken to the monastery to escape the *streltsy* rebellion in Moscow and hidden in the Dormition church behind the iconostasis.

WHAT TO DO

After a day of sightseeing, there are still plenty of things to see and do. Despite high costs, shopping provides many pleasures and plenty of bargains. Parks, sporting events and folk festivals are a great way to unwind and indulge in some enlightening people-watching. And in the evening, there's no reason to sit in the hotel channel-surfing: Moscow has more concerts, operas, dance performances, theatre, clubs, dancing and jazz per square mile than almost any other European capital. And the city is remarkably child-friendly, with plenty of activities for youngsters and their parents.

SHOPPING

Moscow used to be the great merchant capital of Russia, and in the past 20 years it has begun to reclaim its legacy. Traditional arcades have been restored and filled with new shops, both Russian and foreign, and malls keep constantly cropping up. For crafts and souvenirs, there's nothing to match Izmaylovo Vernisazh – an enormous flea market set in a fake old Russian fortress.

WHAT TO BUY

Amber and semi-precious stones. The best amber is brilliantly transparent, although green and opaque white amber are also highly prized. Look for jewellery made from Russia's indigenous semi-precious stones, such as malachite, lapis lazuli, and

Bargaining

Bargaining is acceptable within limits: vendors will round down the price or give a discount for a large purchase. But don't expect to haggle down much more than 10–20 percent of the asking price.

Bolshoy Theatre

Fur hats

charoite, a purple stone discovered in the late 20th century by the river Chara.

Ceramics, porcelain and crystal. Blue and white Russian ceramics from Gzhel are of excellent quality and affordable. Fine bone china and porcelain from the Imperial Factory in St Petersburg and Russian crystal are also high-quality.

Food and drink. Vodka (particularly the flavoured varieties) and caviar are good bargains; buy in brand supermarkets (such as Sedmoy Kontinent or Azbuka Vkusa) to ensure quality. Russian chocolates are also splendid and much richer than many Western brands. Try Korkunov or anything from the Red October factory.

Fur. Some visitors like the idea of buying one of the famous fur hats. The best ones are made from fox, mink, sable and karakul wool. Check the seams to be sure they are tight and scrunch the hat to be sure the fur pops up nicely (if it does not, the fur may be dried out or old). Stylish coats made with Russian fur are so expensive that most local people buy furs imported from Turkey, Greece or Italy.

Lacquer boxes. In the Soviet period icon-painters were 're-educated' and began to use their age-old techniques to create magnificent lacquer boxes. The villages of Palekh, Mstera, Fedoskino and Kholuy each have their own styles. To be sure you are buying the real thing, run your finger over the edges of the painting. If it isn't smooth, the image may be an appliqué.

Books. Souvenir picture books, on subjects such as icons and the Kremlin are inexpensive and authoritative.

Linen and woollens. Hand-knitted socks, sweaters and scarves made of angora wool are cheap and toasty warm. Paisley scarves are also a good bargain, but be sure to ask if they are made in Russia (many come from Pakistan and India). Russian table linen is of excellent quality and quite inexpensive, as are clothes made of linen and linen jersey.

Soviet memorabilia. There is a cottage industry in Soviet kitsch, from army surplus to velvet banners promising a bright future for all communists. Check to be sure it is truly old (fresh colours suggest it was made last week). Reproduction Soviet posters also make good souvenirs. Remember that anything over 50 years old cannot be exported.

Toys and dolls. *Matryoshka* (nesting) dolls come in all sizes and designs, from traditional peasant women to political figures. Carved wooden toys and Christmas tree decorations make delightful gifts.

Souvenir shopping

WHERE TO SHOP

ARTISAN AND SOUVENIR MARKETS

Every weekend the main draw for tourist shoppers is the Izmaylovo Vernisazh (Sat–Sun 9am–6pm, many booths also open on weekdays; metro Partizanskaya), a huge outdoor market with hundreds of booths selling items from Soviet kitsch to rare antiques. Artists sell their paintings on the river embankment by the New Tretyakov Gallery, and there is a crafts market in front of the building which is smaller (and cheaper) than Izmaylovo.

BUYING ART

Over the past few years Moscow's contemporary art scene has become increasingly lively and more interesting. Although there is no art quarter, Winzavod (4-y Syromyatnichesky pereulok 1, str. 6; www.winzavod.ru), a reconstructed 19th-century wine factory, has become a hub for the city's most innovative galleries, most notably the Guelman Galleries. The Central House of Artists (Krymsky val 10/14) has a plethora of small shops and galleries. The former Red October Chocolate Factory on Bolotny Island has a number of cutting-edge galleries showing contemporary Russian artists and photographers. The NB Gallery (Filippovsky pereulok 6/2, apt. 2; www.nbgallery.ru) represents a variety of artists and styles. M'ARS Center (Pushkaryov pereulok 5; www.centermars.com) features cutting-edge contemporary artists and exhibitions. All serious galleries provide Ministry of Culture permission to export the art (and will usually ship items to the customer). Artists of lesser renown also sell their work on the Arbat and at Izmaylovo. Works purchased for under $100 are usually not questioned at customs (although customs officials have considerable discretion in their determinations), so ask for a receipt, even handwritten, for any art you purchase.

DEPARTMENT STORES

The main department stores have mostly foreign shops, but are attractive places to visit. GUM (State Department Store; Krasnaya ploshchad 3; www.gum.ru; daily 10am–10pm), is airy and light, with a beautiful fountain (a traditional meeting place). Souvenirs and Russian ware are on the second floor. TsUM (Central Department Store; Petrovka 2; daily 10am–10pm) is an upmarket department store. Just up

Yeliseev's Emporium, a style moderne food shop

the street at Petrovka 10 is Petrovsky Passazh, a *style moderne* arcade with upscale shopping and dining.

GIFT AND SOUVENIR SHOPS

There are a number of shops in the city centre with good-quality crafts and unusual gifts. In the Historical Museum on Red Square (Krasnaya ploshchad ½) is a store of particularly high-quality crafts and souvenirs. The lobby of the Central House of Artists (Krymsky val 10/14) has a number of boutiques selling art books, crafts, and affordable original art. Not far from the Bolshoy Theatre is the Russkiye Suveniry shop (Ulitsa Petrovka 17, str. 7), which is packed from floor to ceiling with artisans' works. The Russian Souvenirs shop (Palashevsky pereulok 6) offers all kinds of traditional Russian hand-made gifts. On Bolotny Island in the Red October complex there are several showrooms offering cutting-edge Russian fashion and jewellery (Bersenevskaya

DVDs

Russian DVD discs are formatted in regional code 5. You'll need multi-system players in order to view them.

nab. 6, str. 1, tel: 499-788 6000). On Arbat, there are dozens of shops selling traditional crafts, posters, and jewellery.

PRINT AND ELECTRONIC GOODS

Dom Knigi (Novy Arbat 8), Moskva (Tverskaya ulitsa 8), and Biblio Globus (Myasnitskaya ulitsa 6) all have large selections of art books and posters. Dom Knigi and the Delikatesy stereo stores scattered about the city also have a large selection of DVDs, as well as licensed computer programmes, music and films. Discs sold on the street, in kiosks and at the electronics markets are generally pirated. The music store Transylvania (Ulitsa Tverskaya 6/1, str. 5, in the courtyard to the north adjoining Kamergersky pereulok) has an enormous selection of Russian music, from classical to contemporary.

BATH HOUSES

For quintessential Russian R&R, head to the bath house (баня – *banya*). Bring flip-flops, bathing essentials and toiletries. Buy a ticket and ask for a sheet (простыня – *prostynya*), towel (полотенце – *polotenste*), and bag check (хранение – *khranenie*). You might also buy a felt hat (шляпа – *shlyapa*) and bough of branches (веник – *venik*). In the steam room, novices should sit on the bottom bench where the heat is lowest. From the steam room, head for the cold water pool and plunge in. Once you're refreshed, you can go back into the steam room where you can have an attendant pound you to improve your circulation. The usual ritual is several steams interspersed with pampering procedures and breaks for tea, mineral water, or beer and snacks.

ENTERTAINMENT AND NIGHTLIFE

Moscow has a vibrant nightlife that caters to all tastes. Performances usually begin at 7pm, precluding a pre-theatre dinner, but there are stalls in virtually all the theatres and concert halls that open before the performance and during intermissions, selling sandwiches, drinks and pastries. The audience arrives, wearing everything from work clothes to jeans to evening dress. Coats and large bags must be checked. Tickets can be purchased at theatre box offices, theatre kiosks around the city, through hotel service desks or at www.parter.ru. Touts usually have tickets furtively for sale at the prime venues.

DANCE

Ballet has been performed in Moscow since the 1730s. Today the best troupes are in the Bolshoy Theatre and the Kremlin

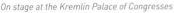
On stage at the Kremlin Palace of Congresses

Palace of Congresses. The Moskva Russian Chamber Ballet has two troupes that perform both traditional and modern ballets on several stages throughout the city. The Kinetic Theatre, a modern dance troupe led by Alexandr Pepelyaev, is worth seeing when they're in town. The New Ballet has a small permanent stage, where they perform dance pieces that include ballet, pantomime and drama. For folk dance, the Moiseyev troupe is the best and often performs in the capital. Keep your eye out for billboards advertising visiting guest troupes, especially from the former Soviet republics.

OPERA AND MUSIC

Opera-lovers will find much joy in Moscow. The Bolshoy repertory and productions are quite traditional, but the Gelikon Opera House has two small stages where their troupes perform operas in unusual productions and a variety of

Great Hall of the Moscow Conservatory

lesser-known Russian and foreign operas. The New Opera performs a mixed repertory in a beautifully renovated hall, and after years of restoration, the Stanislavsky and Nemerovich-Danchenko Musical Theatre is again open and performing opera, ballet and other concerts.

If you are interested in unusual chamber pieces, don't miss the small, but brilliant, Pokrovsky Moscow Chamber Musical Theatre. And if you

---

Opera greats

If you want to experience the majesty and power of Russian opera – glorious music, the pageantry of Russian history, magnificent sets, huge choirs and those booming Russian basses – see *Boris Godunov* and *Khovanshchina* by Modest Mussorgsky (1839–81), *The Queen of Spades* and *Yevgeny Onegin* by Petr Tchaikovsky (1840–93) and *Ruslan and Lyudmila* by Mikhail Glinka (1804–57).

---

are in the mood for light opera and musicals, there is the Moscow Operetta Theatre.

The finest hall for classical music is the Great Hall of the Moscow Conservatory, with its heavenly acoustics and old world elegance. For chamber concerts and performances by soloists, check the schedule of the Conservatory's two other spaces, the Small Hall and the Rachmaninov Hall. The Tchaikovsky Concert Hall is home to the Moscow State Academic Philharmonic and the venue for the Moscow Symphony Orchestra and a variety of musical and dance performances. The newest concert hall is the comfortable Moscow International House of Music.

During the summer the Arkhangelskoe, Tsaristyno and Ostankino estates host chamber concerts in their elegant halls. Throughout the year, the Tretyakov Gallery, the Pushkin Museum of Fine Arts, the Pushkin Literary Museum, and many of the city's apartment-museums also hold concerts in their galleries and museum halls.

THEATRE

A scene from the play 'The Cripple of Inishmaan'

Ever since Stanislavsky and Nemerovich-Danchenko changed the world of drama with their Moscow Art Theatre, Moscow has been one of the great capitals of the stage, even during the Soviet years. If you don't know Russian but are mad about theatre, try seeing a play you know well (Chekhov or Shakespeare). You will rarely miss at the Sovremennik, Lenkom, the Theatre on Malaya Bronnaya, or the two stages of the Moscow Art Theatre. For Russian classics in a beautiful theatre, go to the Maly Theatre. For innovation, take in the Fomenko Studio Theatre.

POPULAR MUSIC AND CLUBS

Muscovites have been jazz fiends since the first bands appeared in 1922. Today there are more than a dozen clubs where jazz is performed regularly, including Forte (Bolshaya Bronnaya ulitsa 18), the Jazz Art Club (Pyatnitskaya ulitsa 27) and Igor Butman Club (Verkhnaya Radischevskaya ulitsa 21). There is a nice piano bar, doubling as a restaurant, with home-cooked food at one of old Moscow apartments (Bolshaya Nikitskaya 22/2). The club scene changes constantly, but B2 (Bolshaya Sadovaya ulitsa 8), Gogol (Stoleshnikov pereulok 11) and 16 Tons (Presnensky Val 6, str. 1) draw crowds year after year. For a classic nightclub, it's the Night Flight (Tverskaya ulitsa 17), which has not closed its doors since opening in 1991. For a glimpse at the young and wealthy, spend the night club-hopping on Bolotny Island. Most clubs have an entry fee and some have face control. Check local listings (see page 127) and www.expat.ru for special events and current hot spots.

SPORTS

SPECTATOR SPORTS

Russians are avid football and hockey fans, divided in their loyalties between Dinamo, CSKA, Spartak and Lokomotiv. Tickets can be purchased at the stadiums or through online services like www.parter.ru or www.sport-tiket.ru. Fans can get rowdy, so expect lots of mounted militia – and wear the right team colours.

ACTIVE SPORTS

In the winter several of the city parks flood their paths and broadcast music over the loudspeakers. Favourite venues are the Hermitage Gardens (Karetny ryad 3), Sokolniki (Sokolnichesky val 3), the GUM rink on Red Square, and Gorky Park.

During the warm months (usually the end of April to September, depending on the weather) boats ply the Moscow River with stops at various points within and outside the city. Tickets and boarding are by Kievsky train station; longer trips to Khimki reservoir, Gorki

In winter, everyone gets their skates on

and Bukhta radosti leave from Rechnoy vokzal. At VVTs (All-Russian Exhibition Centre) you can hire skates by the hour. You can also hire a table, paddles and balls for table tennis by the main fountain, or a boat to paddle about the pond at the far corner of the park (straight back from the entrance), or bicycles.

And if you need to release some urban aggression, there's a paint-ball playground near the pond.

ACTIVITIES FOR CHILDREN

Moscow has a variety of entertainment for the junior set, particularly if they like animals.

Zoo (Bolshaya Gruzinskaya ulitsa 1, tel: 495-252 3580, www. moscowzoo.ru). Still a bit old-style, but with some guaranteed crowd-pleasers for kids.

Circus on Tsvetnoy (Tvernoy bulvar 13, tel: 495-621 1403). Great fun for animal- and circus-lovers of all ages. Bring extra cash to have your photo taken with trained animals.

'New Circus' (Prospekt Vernadskovo 7, tel: 495-930 0300, www.greatcircus.ru). Larger than the 'old' circus on Tvetnoy bulvar, but with the same high quality.

Children's Musical Theatre (Vernadskovo prospekt 5, tel: 495-120 2515). Great repertory of musicals for kids with costumed actors who entertain the audience before the show.

Durov's Corner (Ulitsa Durova 4, tel: 495-631 3047) has extraordinary acts with all kinds of creatures – all trained with the Durov family's 'loving' (non-violent) approach.

Kuklyachyov Cat Theatre (Kutuzovsky prospekt 25, tel: 499-243 4005, www.kuklachev.ru). Trained felines and clowns perform.

Obraztsov Puppet Theatre (Sadovaya-Samotechnaya ulitsa 3, tel: 495-699 5373, www.puppet.ru). Classical and modern puppet shows.

CALENDAR OF EVENTS

Dates and festivals change from year to year, depending on funding and availability of stars and venues. Here are the main events by season:

Winter: December to March. The Pushkin Museum holds concerts called December Evenings in their halls throughout the month. Special concert series are held every year before and after Russian Orthodox Christmas (7 January) and many city parks celebrate the season with troika (sleigh) rides and other cold-weather merriment. The week before Lent is called Maslenitsa (Butter Week), a weeklong splurge of *blinys* and vodka before the strict Lenten fast. Pancakes, honey-wine and festivities are enjoyed every night by St Basil's Cathedral, and on the last weekend before Lent most of the palaces and parks hold traditional games and contests.

Spring: April and May. After Easter, conductor Valery Gergiev hosts the Moscow Easter Festival (www.easterfestival.ru).

Summer: June to August. In June Moscow is host to the annual Moscow International Film Festival (www.moscowfilmfestival.ru). Every other summer the city hosts the Chekhov International Theatre Festival (www.chekhovfest.ru). The prestigious International Tchaikovsky Competition (http://tchaikovskycompetition.com) is held every fourth year. The Hermitage Gardens are the site of an ethnic music festival (usually early July) and a Jazz Festival (late August). City palaces hold music festivals throughout the summer.

Autumn: September to November. City Day is celebrated on the weekend closest to 6 September, with music, parades and outdoor fun throughout Moscow. On the first Sunday in September, the Battle of Borodino is re-fought at the site of the original battle (tours arranged by Patriarshy Dom, see page 123). The Kremlin Cup Tennis Tournament is held in early October. The Moscow Biennale (www.moscowbiennale.ru) has been drawing increased attention between September and October of odd-numbered years since 2003.

EATING OUT

Russians are serious about good food and good company. In fact, one little word – застолье *(zastolye)* – encompasses the pleasure of sitting at the table for a long evening, enjoying good food and drink, excellent and witty conversation, plenty of toasts, and a song or two. It's not surprising that as soon as it became possible, thousands of restaurants and cafés appeared in Moscow with an extraordinary range of cuisines and special attention to décor, ambiance, music – and even to the restrooms, which are, in the most elegant restaurants, the most spectacularly decorated rooms in the space. Traditional Russian cooking is peasant-hearty, based on readily available root vegetables and fish. But under the tsars it was also heavily influenced by French cuisine, and it is now being revived in imaginative recipes that borrow from a wealth of traditions, especially from the

Café Pushkin

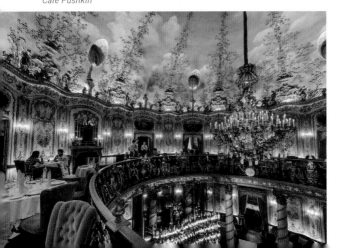

former Soviet republics to the east and south.

Breakfast is usually served from about 7am to noon. The lunch hour stretches from noon to 4pm, and dinner is usually served from 6–11pm (sometimes until the last customer), although most restaurants only get crowded

> **No, thanks**
>
> Many Russian dishes are served with sour cream and sprinkled liberally with dill. If you wish your dish to be garnish-free, say 'No sour cream' (без сметаны – bez smetany) or 'No dill' (без укропа – bez ukropa).

after 7 or 8pm (call ahead for reservations for dining after 8pm and to clarify the eatery's credit card policy; in most cases, you'll need to bring cash). All day long you can stop in a coffee shop (кофейня – kofeynya) for coffee, tea and sweet and savoury treats.

WHERE TO EAT

There is a reasonable choice of restaurants right across the city. Pasta and sushi restaurants offer the most popular foreign cuisines. Several Russian fast-food chains – Yolki-palki, Moo-Moo, and Teremok – provide decent food, beer and wine at affordable prices. The Old and New Arbat, the Okhotny Ryad underground shopping mall by the Aleksandrovsky Gardens and Kamergersky pereulok (between Tverskaya ulitsa and Bolshaya Dmitrovka) all have dozens of restaurants and cafés. Consider trying the cuisines of Georgia, Armenia, Uzbekistan, or Belarus – all are amply represented in Moscow. Virtually all restaurants and many cafés have English menus, even if the dishes are somewhat whimsically translated. During the day, look for бизнес-ланч (business lunch); these are fixed price meals of starter, soup, main course and coffee or beverage that are an excellent bargain.

BREAKFAST

For a Russian breakfast (завтрак – *zavtrak*), try porridge (каша – *kasha*), cheese pancakes (сырники – *syrniki*) served with sour cream (сметана – *smetana*) and jam. Russians love dairy products and serve cottage cheese (творог – *tvorog*), yoghurt (йогурт – *iogurt*), and lassi (кефир – *kefir*) at breakfast. You might also be offered an omelette (омлет – *omlette*) or fried eggs (яичница – *yaichnitsa*). Be sure to sample the rich dark bread (чёрный – *chyorny*); Бородинский – *Borodinsky* is a dense dark bread sprinkled with dill seeds.

LUNCH AND SUPPER

Russians traditionally eat their largest meal of the day at lunchtime, though the pressures of the workplace are changing this. Lunch (обед – *obed*) usually consists of a starter (закуски – *zakuski*) and/or salad (салат – *salat*), soup (суп – *sup*), a main course (второе – *vtoroye*) and dessert (сладкое – *sladkoe*). The best food deal is the set-price business lunch (бизнес-ланч – *biznes-lanch*). At home the evening meal (ужин – *uzhin*) is often much lighter than lunch and might be a salad or open-faced sandwich (бутерброд – *buterbrod*). But evening meals in restaurants tend to be lavish with course after course enjoyed to the accompaniment of stories, songs and much talking. At the end of the meal is tea (чай – *chay*) with lemon and sugar, and a rich cake (торт – *tort*).

Steamed fish at Yar restaurant

ZAKUSKI AND SALADS

The best part of a Russian meal is the first course, *zakuski* – salads, sliced smoked meats, smoked and salted fish, fresh and pickled vegetables, salted and marinated mushrooms, and puff pastries (пирожки – *pirozhki*) filled with meat, potatoes, mushrooms, sautéed cabbage or fish. A holiday table might have a dozen different dishes; a restaurant table for a celebratory crowd might have half a dozen. A good choice for a light meal is one or two of these delectable dishes. Russian salads include both fresh vegetables, traditionally cucumbers and tomatoes (or radishes) seasoned with dill with a sour cream dressing,

Caviar at Volkhonka Mansion

and elaborate and complex dishes made of dozens of ingredients (and often with uninformative names, such as 'surprise' or 'Moscow'; ask the staff for a description). The classic mixed salad (винегрет – *vinegret*) is made of beetroot, potatoes, carrots and pickles dressed with oil, mayonnaise or sour cream. Almost every restaurant has a version of the Salad Olivier (салат Оливье), made of potatoes, onions, pickles and thin strips of meat (chicken, tongue or beef), and dressed with mayonnaise.

The lakes and rivers of Russia teem with hundreds of kinds of fish, and cooks have devised thousands of ways of preparing them. The *zakuski* table almost always includes herring (селёдка – *selyodka*), served with fresh onions and boiled potatoes, or the fancifully named 'herring under a fur coat' (селёдка под шубой – *selyodka pod shuboi*), herring buried

Kharcho, a meaty soup that originates from Georgia

under a rich salad of beetroot, potatoes, boiled egg and sour cream. Russian smoked fish is excellent (sturgeon, salmon, trout or cod) along with servings of sprats, or fish in aspic (заливное из рыбы – *zalivnoe iz ryby*). At least once you should splurge on pancakes (блины – *bliny*) with caviar (икра – *ikra*). Connoisseurs consider *malossol*, the delicate bluish-grey, lightly salted Beluga caviar, to be the best, although *ossetra* (stronger in flavour) or *sevruga* (a strong, nutty flavour) have their fans. Red salmon roe (красная икра – *krasnaya ikra*) has large red grains with a strong and salty flavour.

For meat lovers, there is veal or beef in aspic (холодец – *kholdets*) served with ferociously hot horseradish, or a selection of smoked sausages (колбаса – *kolbasa*) and smoked meats (копченье – *kopchene*). Vegetarians might enjoy a dish called Julienne (жюльен – *zhyulen*), a little pot of sliced mushrooms served in a white sauce topped with cheese and served bubbling hot from the oven.

SOUPS

Every visitor to Moscow needs to have at least one hearty bowl of borscht (борщ), even though this soup is actually Ukrainian. There are as many recipes as cooks; it is sometimes made with mushrooms or even prunes, and is traditionally served with hot rolls called *pampushki* (пампушки), which are drizzled with garlic sauce. Other hearty soups include *pokhlyobki* (похлёбки) made from meat, poultry or fish with onions, potatoes and carrots, and the complex *solyanka* (солянка), a thick and slightly sour soup made with mushrooms, fish or meat and seasoned with pickles, olives, capers and lemon and topped with sour cream. Lighter soups include mushroom (грибной – *gribnoy*), with strongly fla-voured field mushrooms, most commonly porcini; a light fish soup (уха – *ukha*) that is a delicate broth seasoned with potatoes, carrots and onions; or clear chicken soups (куриная лапша – *kurinaya lapsha*). For good peasant fare, try the cabbage soup (щи – *shchi*), made with fresh cabbage or sauerkraut, a vegeta-ble or meat broth and seasoned with a dollop of sour cream. Classic summer soups include *okroshka* (окрошка), an unusual soup made of *kvas* (квас), a mildly alcoholic drink derived from black bread and ladled over diced vegetables, or a clear beet-root soup (свекольник – *svekolnik*), which is ladled over a salad

VEGETARIAN SELECTION

Vegetarians are always happy during one of the year's four major reli-gious fasts: menus in finer restaurants include a special menu without meat, fish or dairy products (постное меню – *postnoe menyu*). But dur-ing the rest of the year, there are plenty of dishes for even strict veg-etarians: fresh vegetable salads, creamed vegetable soups (овощной суп-пюре – *ovoshchnoy sup-pyure*), potato-filled dumplings (вареники с картофелем – *vareniki s kartofelem*) and dozens of dishes made with mushrooms. Identify yourself as a vegetarian (вегетарианец – *vegetar-ianets*) and ask the serving staff for help. The ethnic cuisines offer many tasty options, too. And if you are ravenous on the street, you can always buy a puff pastry filled with cheese (слойка с сыром – *sloika s syrom*) at one of the stalls. There are also fruit and vegetable stalls scattered about the city, usually at major intersections or at stations. Fruit and vegetables should be washed well, but are usually fresh and especially delicious in the warm months when they are locally grown.

Desserts

At the end of your meal, try *kisel* (кисель), a traditional soft jelly of fruits and thickened with cornflour, and rich ice cream (мороженое/*morozhenoe*), or splurge on a Napoleon cake: layers of puff pastry with a rich cream filling, apparently created for the French emperor.

of potatoes, cucumbers and radishes dressed with sour cream and seasoned with dill or parsley.

MAIN DISHES

After the complexity of the *zakuski*, diners tend to choose simply sautéed, grilled or roast meat or fish. For a classic Russian main course, try *pelmeni* (пельмени), the Russian version of ravioli made of a mixture of pork, beef and/or lamb wrapped in pasta dough, or stuffed cabbage (голубцы – *golubsty*), usually served in a tomato-based sauce. For memories of Imperial Russia, try beef stroganov in a rich sour cream sauce, or pre-Revolutionary dishes made of venison, boar, suckling pig, goose or duck. Fish are grilled (на гриле – *na grille*), fried (жареная – *zharenaya*), baked (тушеная – *tushenaya*) or fried in batter (в кляре – *v klyare*). Sturgeon is particularly delicious grilled.

In most restaurants you order garnishes (гарнир – *garnir*) separately, from a choice that usually includes vegetables (овощи – *ovoshchi*), fries (картофель фри – *kartofel fri*), mashed potatoes (картофельное пюре – *kartofelnoe pyure*) or buckwheat (гречневая каша – *grechnevaya kasha*).

CUISINES FROM THE SOUTH AND EAST

While in Moscow, you might sample cuisines from the former Soviet republics: there are dozens of Georgian, Armenian, Azeri and Uzbek restaurants in the capital. Cuisine from the Caucasus is spicier than Russian food, with dozens of salads and dishes made with aubergines (баклажаны – *baklazhany*) and fresh vegetables. Georgian cuisine is famous for its lamb dumplings (хинкали – *khinkali*), spicy pureed beans (лобио – *lobio*), and cheese pies (хачапури – *khachapuri*). All the southern cuisines prepare tasty shish-kebabs (шашлык – *shashlyk*), which Russians have adopted as a national dish. Uzbek cuisine is famous for its pilafs (плов – *plov*) and rich soups.

WHAT TO DRINK

At table you might want to try *mors* (морс), a refreshing drink made of fresh berries mixed with sugar and water, or traditional mineral water. Russians accompany their *zakuski* with chilled vodka drunk straight: try a flavoured one such as lemon or pepper and honey. To stay on your feet, do as the Russians do: after a gulp of vodka, immediately take a mouthful of salad or appetiser, or drink down some *mors*. Russians also produce and drink good beer (пиво – *pivo*), often with crayfish or shrimp to munch on, or bread coated with garlic and fried (сухарики – *sukhariki*). Russians import more wine every year. From the south of the country come decent wines and good sparkling wine – шампанское (*shampanskoe*) – though it can be difficult to find brut (брют) or dry (сухое – *sukhoe*). Some restaurants are reviving pre-Revolutionary drinks, such as *sbiten* (сбитень), a hot fermented drink made of honey

Vodka

and spices, and *medovukha* (медовуха), a spiced honey-wine. Armenian cognacs are drunk straight, like vodka, with a slice of lemon.

TO HELP YOU ORDER...

Is there a table free? Есть свободный столик? **Est svobodny stolik?**

I'd like... Мне... **Mne...**

Waiter/menu официант/меню **ofitsiant/menyu**

The bill, please Посчитайте, пожалуйста. **Poschitayte, pozhaluysta.**

bread хлеб **khleb**

butter масло **maslo**

coffee кофе **kofe**

dessert сладкое **sladkoe**

fish рыба **ryba**

fruit фрукты **frukti**

ice cream мороженое **morozhenoe**

meat мясо **myaso**

milk молоко **moloko**

pepper перец **perets**

potatoes картофель **kartofel**

rice рис **ris**

salad салат **salat**

salt соль **sol**

sandwich бутерброд **buterbrod**

soup суп **sup**

sugar сахар **sakhar**

wine вино **vino**

... AND READ THE MENU

porridge каша **kasha**

frankfurter сосиска **sosiska**

smoked/boiled sausage копчёная/варёная колбаса
  kopchyonaya/var-yonaya kolbasa

pancake/blini блины **bliny**

stuffed blini блинчики **blinchiki**

potato salad салат ЂСтоличныйЋ **salat 'Stolichny'**

green salad зелёный салат **zelyony salat**

fresh vegetables свежие овощи **svezhie ovoshchi**

assorted fish/smoked meats рыбное/мясное ассорти
  rybnoe/myasnoe assorti

marinated mushrooms маринованные грибы
  marinovannye griby

beef/veal говядина/телятина **govyadina/telyatina**

pork свинина **svinina**

cutlets котлеты **kotlety**

lamb баранина **baranina**

venison оленина **olenina**

horsemeat (a Central Asian delicacy) конина **konina**

chicken курица/цыплёнок **kuritsa/tsyplyonok**

duck утка **utka**

goose гусь **gus**

cod треска **treska**

trout форель **forel**

sturgeon осетрина **osetrina**

young sturgeon стерлядь **sterlyad**

crayfish раки **raki**

shrimp креветки **krevetki**

grilled на гриле **na grile**

fresh (pl) свежие **svezhie**

smoked (pl) копчёные **kopchyonye**

fried/sautéed (pl) жареные **zharenye**

baked/roasted (pl) тушёные **tushyonye**

stuffed (pl) фаршированные **farshirovannye**

pastry пирожное **pirozhnoe**

PLACES TO EAT

As a guide, we have used the following symbols to give some idea of the cost of a three-course dinner for two. The prices are a US-dollar average, with drinks.

$$$$ over $80   **$$$** $50–80
$$ $30–50   **$** below $30

WITHIN THE GARDEN RING ROAD

AROUND TVERSKAYA AND THE NORTH

Belaya Rus $–$$ *Bolshaya Nikitskaya ulitsa 14, tel: 495-629 4176.* Located in a cellar, this café with white brick walls stencilled in folk patterns serves hearty, inexpensive peasant fare from Belarus. Try the pork in aspic with horseradish, *solyanka* soups, homemade sausages and *draniki* – fried potato pancakes served with a variety of toppings.

Central House of Writers $$$$ *Povarskaya ulitsa 50, tel: 495-291 1515.* Elegant Russian and Italian cuisine served in the soaring, wood-panelled hall of a 19th-century mansion. Extravagant updates of traditional Russian food, such as elk *pelmeni*, or quail stuffed with chestnuts and served with risotto from an extensive Italian menu.

Coffeemania $$ *Bolshaya Nikitskaya ulitsa 13, tel: 495-775 5188, www. coffeemania.ru.* Coffeemania has several locations about the city, but the one next to the Conservatory is open 24 hours and has a particularly pleasant summer terrace. The chain has a good pan-European menu with a delectable assortment of pastries and sweets.

Godunov $$–$$$ *Teatralnaya ploshchad 5/1, tel: 495-698 4490, www. godunov.net.* Right off Red Square in a renovated section of a 17th-century monastery building, this restaurant serves good Russian and European cuisine in rooms painted like a boyar's hall. Touristy, but fun atmosphere and good food.

Khachapuri $ *Bolshoy Gnezdnikovsky pereulok, 10, tel: 495-629 6656, www.hacha.ru.* This Georgian café, just off Pushkin Square, serves tasty national specialities, with a particularly good variety of *khachapuri*, a cheese bread that gave its name to the restaurant. No alcohol, but excellent homemade, flavoured fizzy water.

Margarita $–$$ *Malaya Bronnaya ulitsa 28, tel: 495-699 6534.* Café Margarita is one of Moscow's first and oldest private restaurants, which started as a cheap café and has turned into a neighbourhood legend. It is a tiny café with dark wood, knick-knacks and lots of references to Bulgakov's novel, *The Master and Margarita* (which had key scenes set at nearby Patriarch's Pond). It serves tasty Russian food, with some European dishes thrown in. Every night there is live music: classical musicians playing jazz, rock, folk and whatever they wish on violins and piano.

Mari Vanna $$ *Spiridonevsky pereulok 10a, tel: 495-650 6500.* Russian home-cooking in a convincingly informal Russian apartment atmosphere, complete with a resident cat and dog. Excellent homemade fruit liqueurs. Reservations strongly recommended.

Praga $$$–$$$$ *Ulitsa Arbat 2/1, tel: 495-690 6171.* Before the 1917 Revolution the Praga restaurant was one of Moscow's finest, where professors, musicians and writers enjoyed elegant dining in the extravagantly decorated halls. Today these over-the-top halls in Russian, Japanese, European, Eastern and Brazilian motifs match the wildly varied menus. The traditional Russian menu, including recipes from its pre-Revolutionary incarnation, is the best, particularly the authentic borscht with rolls dripping with garlic, and the sautéed pheasant with homemade loganberry sauce. Celebrated desserts include chocolate cream Praga cake and the ethereal 'Bird's Milk' cake – invented by the resident chef and named for the unattainable delicacy of Russian fairy tales.

Pushkin Café $$$–$$$$ *Tverskoy bulvar 26a, tel: 495-739 0033,* www.cafe-pushkin.ru. Some of the best Russian cuisine in Moscow is to be had in this artfully restored manor house. Traditional dishes are revitalised and complemented by European-inspired fare. Reservations essential, as the lunch and dinner crowds are filled with local celebrities.

Starlite Diner $–$$ *Bolshaya Sadovaya 16a, tel: 495-650 0246,* www.starlite.ru. A classic US diner. The stainless steel train-carriage venue seems to have been beamed rivet by rivet to the Aquarium Garden near Mayakovskaya metro. It has booths, circa 1970s *Life* and *Look* covers on the walls, bobby-socked waitresses and surprisingly good home-style American and Russian food. It's the favourite expat Sunday brunch joint and open 24 hours.

Tchaikovsky $–$$ *Triumfalnaya ploshchad 4/31, tel: 495-699 9114*. Located in the vestibule of the Tchaikovsky Concert Hall, this sprawling elegant café offers everything from breakfast blinis and good European coffee to pre- and post-concert drinks with *pelmeni* or an apple tart.

Yolki-Palki $–$$ *Ulitsa Novy Arbat 11, tel: 495-785 3875*. This chain of restaurants has a dozen branches about the city. All provide decent quality fast food in an *à la russe* rustic décor. The all-you-can eat salad bar is a good bargain, and the main courses, like *pelmeni*, while not haute cuisine, are tasty and satisfying. All the branches take credit cards.

10 Cafe $$ *Bolshaya Sadovaya ulitsa 10, tel: 499-130 8242*, www10cafe. ru. International street food classics served in upmarket surroundings with a huge selection of alcoholic and non-alcoholic beverages.

13 $$ *4-aya Tverskaya-Yamskaya ulitsa 13, tel: 915-206 9449*. Simply furnished, but charming wine bar with a great selection of wines and a simple menu of grilled fish and steaks plus salads.

AROUND PETROVKA

Barashka $$$ *Ulitsa Petrovka 20/1 (entrance on Petrovskie linii), tel: 495-228 3730*, www.novikovgroup.ru. This elegant, cleanly designed restaurant serves authentic and stylishly presented Azeri cuisine. They are renowned for their kababs and *plov* (served in layers), as well as *dyushbara* (tiny dumplings in a herby broth).

Beloe Solntse v Pustyne (White Sun of the Desert) $$$ *Neglinnaya ulitsa 29/14, tel: 495-625 2596*, www.novikovgroup.ru. A theme restaurant based on a popular 1969 Soviet film, this place has a kitschy atmosphere, high prices, but excellent Uzbek, Azeri, 'Arabic' and Chinese specialities. Locals consider their range of *plov* the best in the city.

Kitezhgrad $$$ *Ulitsa Petrovka 23/10, tel: 495-650 6685, www.kitezh-town.ru.* Named after a Russian fairy tale city, Kitezhgrad has a rustic village interior and serves hearty traditional and updated Russian cuisine, including a good selection of *bliny* and *pelmeni* (with duck and fish), and a lavish hunter's menu of bear, venison, pheasant and wild boar.

Mayak $-$$ *Bolshaya Nikitskaya ulitsa 19, entrance on side street, second floor, tel: 495-691 7449.* Unpretentious, airy bistro with Russian and European cuisine and friendly service. A good place for a break from heavy dining, with excellent salads and grilled fish and meat.

The Most $$$$ *Kuznetsky Most 6/3, tel: 495-660 0706, www.brasseriemost.ru.* The Most (a play on the Russian street name, which means 'bridge', and the English superlative) may be the most luxurious restaurant in the city, with a main room in pale cream and pink that looks like an upscale bordello, and a second room that recreates a book-lined study. The menu is divided between 'classical' and 'creative', with unusual combinations (mango and beet salad) and exquisite presentation. Reservations suggested.

Scandinavia $$$$ *Maly Palashevsky pereulok 7, tel: 495-937 5630, www.scandinavia.ru.* Expat and local gourmands consistently rate this as one of Moscow's best restaurants. Excellent updated Scandinavian fare, good service, and a divine summer café located on a narrow side street just off Pushkin Square. For a more modest meal, they have an affordable business lunch, and their burger has been voted the best in the city.

Turandot $$$$ *Tverskoy bulvar 26, tel: 495-739 0011, www.turandot-palace.ru.* A Pan-Asian restaurant with a lot of Chinese and Japanese dishes on the menu, serving excellent sushi. Excellent traditional Russian cuisine is also served here. Palatial interiors plus a lovely roof terrace. Reservations suggested.

Vinoteca Dissident $$$ *Nautilus Shopping Centre, fifth floor, Lubyanka ploshchad, tel: 495-500 2767.* The Dissident is a great venue: tile floors, Eastern rugs, bright furniture with a fabulous view of Lubyanka Square. It is also an excellent wine bar, with more than 200 wines by bottle or glass and an international menu with emphasis on Spanish and Mediterranean cuisine designed to be nibbled with the drinks. The light salads, homemade terrines and patés and excellent cheese boards make this a good place to stop for a pick-me-up after traipsing the city centre.

5642 Visota $$ *Bolshoi Cherkassky pereulok 15-17, tel: 495-624 9321*, www.novikovgroup.ru. Serves delicious and authentic Georgian dishes; the service very good. The name of the restaurant is inspired by the height of the summit of Mount Elbrus – the highest point in Russia and Europe.

AROUND CHISTYE PRUDY & THE NORTHEAST

Avocado $–$$ *Chistoprudny bulvar 12/2, tel: 495-621 7719*. A mix of vegetarian dishes from Asia through Europe to Latin America in an appropriately soothing, non-smoking environment.

Bulka $–$$ *Pokrovka 19, tel: 495-624 9557*, www.bulkabakery.ru. Excellent bakery, patisserie and restaurant. Simple Russian and eastern European dishes served in a cosy ambiance.

Filial $$ *Krivokolenny pereulok 3, str. 1, tel: 495-621 2143*, www.filial moscow.com. A refreshing fusion of various European cuisines served in unpretentious ambience. A live DJ plays several times a week.

Noev Kovcheg (Noah's Ark) $$$–$$$$ *Maly Ivanovsky pereulok 7 9/1, tel: 495-917 0717*. Excellent Armenian cuisine in an upscale and relaxing décor. Try the *kare-kiufta*, a spicy meatball served in Armenian bread *lavash*, the tender *tolma*, or one of the *shashlyks*.

Simple Pleasures $$$–$$$$ *Ulitsa Sretenka 22/1, tel: 495-607 1521*. International and fusion cuisine that is light and imaginative, served in an airy hall or a pleasant patio during the summer months. A mixed clientele of expats and Russians frequent this restaurant, which is in an old neighbourhood now undergoing gentrification.

AROUND OSTOZHENKA & THE SOUTHWEST

Genatsvale $$$ *Ulitsa Ostozhenka 12/1, tel: 495-695 0401*. These two Georgian restaurants side by side (the VIP side is more elegant and expensive) consistently get voted the best Georgian places in town. Excellent food served in abundance with boisterous and noisy ambiance. Reservations suggested.

SOUTH OF THE RIVER

Correa's $$–$$$ *Bolshaya Ordynka 40, tel: 495-725 6035,* http://eng. correas.ru. Isaac Correa is celebrated as the chef who brought fusion cuisine to Moscow, and then surprised everyone by celebrating good old American cuisine at his deli café (Bolshaya Gruzinskaya 32, str. 1). The light and clean décor of his restaurant on Bolshaya Ordynka reflects his style: crispy hand-made pizzas, sumptuous sandwiches and luscious main courses that change every day.

Oblomov $$$$ *1-y Monetchikovsky pereulok 5, tel: 495-953 6828.* Oblomov, named after the main character in a 19th century novel by Ivan Goncharov who lay on his couch, ate, and thought about food for hundreds of pages, is consistently named one of Moscow's best restaurants. Housed in a meticulously restored city mansion, Oblomov offers exquisitely prepared Russian and European cuisine, from the simple pleasure of roasted aubergine caviar to more extravagant culinary adventures, such as bear-meat cutlets. Reservations suggested.

Parka $ *Pyatnitskaya ulitsa 22, tel:* 495-960 8222. An informal restaurant reminiscent of a Russian bathing house – you can sit on stepped benches or at a normal table. Serves a great choice of beers, good burgers and mouth-watering appetizers.

OUTSIDE THE GARDEN RING ROAD

Argumen $$ *Kutuzovsky prospekt 41, tel: 499-249 9955.* Intimate, cosy restaurant-club with 8 tables, serving good, affordable Russian and European cuisine.

Kutuzovskiy 5 $$$$ *Kutuzovsky prospekt 5, tel: 499-243 6540,* www. kutuzovskiy5.ru. A new restaurant specialising in traditional Russian dishes with a modern twist. Exquisite food in an exquisite setting.

Le Restaurant $$$ *2-aya Zvenigorodskaya 13, str. 1, tel: 495-258 2808*. Restaurant from Chef Jean-Luc Molle, serving French dishes with particular emphasis on seafood. The Kamchatka crabs are delicious and the wine selection (French) is excellent.

Sem Pyatnits $$$–$$$$ *Vorontsovskaya ulitsa 6, str. 1, tel: 495-912 1218*. 'Seven Fridays' re-creates a Moscow hotel at the turn of the 20th century, jam-packed with knick-knacks, gramophones and books, and a summer 'theatre' café with tables in a courtyard with mock 19th-century shops. The mostly Russian cuisine is excellent. It has both traditional dishes, including light *blinys*, homemade marinated vegetables and mushrooms, and *pelmeni* stuffed with pork, veal and venison, as well as French-inspired dishes and Moscow 'creative cuisine', such as tuna carpaccio in lime with pesto.

Shinok $$$–$$$$ *Ulitsa 1905 goda 2a, tel: 495-213 8217,* www.shinok. ru. Shinok serves truly excellent Ukrainian food – despite its pricey location by the World Trade Centre and the kitschy glass-covered barnyard with authentic Ukrainian milkmaid. The borscht is authentic, as is the *salo* (spicy uncooked bacon) and *gorilka* (hooch).

U Pirosmani (At Pirosmani's) $$$ *Novodevichiy proezd 4, tel: 499-255 7926*. Excellent Georgian cuisine in a rustic décor overlooking the pond and New Maiden Convent. Strolling violinists in the evening. The salads and *khachapuri* (cheese pies) are particularly delicious, as are the *shashlyk* selections.

Vizir Makhallya & Graf Orlov $$ *2-oy Verkhniy Mikhailovsky proezd 2, tel: 495- 954 0740*. Good and authentic Uzbek food in an elegant décor. Excellent *plov* and *lagman* (a rich noodle) soup, plus a variety of spicy salads. Although it is a bit off the beaten path, it's worth the travel time.

Yar $$$–$$$$ *Leningradsky prospekt 32/2, tel: 495-960 2004,* www. yar-restaurant.ru. Founded in 1826, this was Moscow's finest restaurant until 1917 – the place for elegant dining in the evening and wild gypsy music later on. The present restaurant was remodelled under Stalin and recently done over again. It may no longer be the best in town, but it still provides good Russian food and a rather risqué cabaret show.

A–Z TRAVEL TIPS

A Summary of Practical Information

A

ACCOMMODATION (see also Youth Hostels and the list of Recommended Hotels on page 133)

Moscow's hotels cater largely to a business clientele, and the vast majority of hotels in the city centre are astronomically expensive. However, it seems that every month another modest boutique hotel is opening, and there are now some interesting options for budget travellers. A few Soviet-era hotels and modern three-star hostelries further from the centre also provide more affordable prices but modest accommodation. Another option is short-term apartment rental. Like Home (www.likehome.ru), Four Squares (www.apartments. foursquares.com), and IntermarkSavills (www.intermark.ru) provide serviced apartments, as well as visa support and registration.

Although there is no high or low season in Moscow, the hotels can fill up during the prime conference months of September and April. Most hotels offer sharply discounted weekend rates. Check to see if the quoted rate includes VAT tax (18 percent) and breakfast.

ADDRESSES

Russian addresses require a bit of deciphering. The street is listed first and then the house number (Prospekt Mira 24). An address with a slash in the number, such as Prospekt Mira 24/1, means that it is a

boulevard бульвар **bulvar**
bridge мост **most**
embankment (river) набережная **naberezhnaya**
lane переулок **pereulok**
avenue проспект **prospekt**
square площадь **ploshchad**
highway шоссе **shosse**
street улица **ulitsa**

corner building, number 24 on the main street and number 1 on the perpendicular street. Several buildings can share the same house number but are distinguished by an additional building (строение – *stroenie*) or block (корпус – *korpus*) number. For example, an address might be Prospekt Mira 24, stroenie 4. Another confusion in Moscow is that the two large ring roads, the Boulevard Ring (Бульварное кольцо – Bulvarnoe koltso) and the Garden Ring Road (Садовое кольцо – Sadovoe koltso) have different names for each stretch of road (usually between major crossroads). So Muscovites might tell you that the US Embassy is on the Garden Ring Road, but the address is on Novinsky bulvar, the name of that section of roadway.

AIRPORTS

Moscow has two main international airports, International Airport Sheremetyevo (SVO, www.svo.aero, tel: 495-578 6565 and 925-100 6565) and Domodedovo Airport (DME, www.domodedovo.ru, tel: 495-933 6666). Sheremetyevo is located about 29km (18 miles) to the northwest of the city and Domodedovo is about 40km (25 miles) from the city centre to the south. A third airport, Vnukovo International Airport (VKO, www.vnukovo.ru, tel: 495-937 5555), about 28km (17 miles) to the southwest, is drawing some international airlines.

Transfers. For first-time visitors, it is best to use the airport transfer services provided by your hotel (the fee is about $60) or an official taxi service (about $70) at the airport (booths are in the arrivals hall after baggage claim). Don't use one of the taxi drivers who approach you in the terminal.

All three airports are now served by Aeroexpress (www.aeroexpress.ru; 420 roubles, about $7): the train from Sheremetyevo ends at Belarussian train station. From Domodedovo–Paveletsky train station, and from Vnukovo–Kievsky train station, the trains run every half hour or hour, though not through the night. Schedules can be found on the airport sites.

B

BUDGETING FOR YOUR TRIP

Moscow is one of the world's most expensive cities, but it is afford-able if you stay away from the services in the five-star hotels and foreign establishments.

Transport. Taxis around the city are usually under $10. A car and driver cost $20–100 an hour (depending on the class of car), but one ride on the metro (regardless of distance) is less than $1.

Food. Coffee and a snack at one of the city's ubiquitous coffee shops costs about $7–10, but a soft drink and pastry from a kiosk is about $5. Drinks at an upscale bar can be over $25, but at a modest eatery or pub they are more likely to be $5. Dinner for two (starter, main course and drinks) in one of the many modest restaurants and cafés can be had for $60 or less, although expect to pay twice that in one of the more elegant eateries.

Museums usually have a two-tiered pricing system with higher en-trance and photography fees for foreigners. A full day at the Krem-lin costs about $30, but the entrance fees to smaller museums range from $4–10. It's worthwhile to buy a one, three or five-day Moscow City Pass (www.moscowpass.com), which includes free entrance to many museums, free excursions and discounts at nu-merous bars, restaurants and tourist attractions.

Entertainment. If you don't opt for the best seats, theatre and con-cert tickets are $10–20, and opera and ballet up to $50.

C

CAR RENTAL (see also Driving)

You need to have a credit card, and in most agencies, be over 25 years old. Three trusted companies are Thrifty (Leningradskoe Shosse 65, str.3, 495-788 6888, www.thrifty.com; Biracs Leninsky Prospekt 30, 495-505 2579, www.biracs.ru; and Europcar Vnukovo

Airport international arrival zone, 495-926 6353, www.europcar. com. The average rate is about $150 per day.

A much safer and more pleasant alternative is to hire a car with driver. Most hotels can arrange services. The taxi service Pilot (tel: 495-333 3333, www.taxi-pilot.ru) can provide foreign-made cars with English-speaking drivers at about $70 for 5 hours (although a Russian speaker will have to make the reservation for you).

I'd like to rent a car. Я хочу взять машину напрокат.
Ya khochu vzyat mashinu na prokat.
with a driver/without a driver с водителем/без водителя
s voditelem/bez voditelya
tomorrow на завтра **na zavtra**
for one day/week на один день/на неделю **na odin den/
na nedelyu**

CLIMATE

Muscovites joke about their city's 'moderate continental climate', which means winters can be -30° C (-22° F) and summers can be +30° C (+86° F). In general, spring arrives in April or May; summers are hot and not humid; September can be glorious, but in October the weather gets chillier. By November the trees have

	J	F	M	A	M	J	J	A	S	O	N	D
min												
°C	-8	-9	-5	2	8	12	14	12	8	3	-3	-8
°F	17	16	24	36	46	54	58	54	46	37	26	18
max												
°C	-5	-4	2	11	18	22	24	22	15	8	0	-4
°F	24	25	36	51	65	71	75	71	60	47	32	25

shed their leaves and mud begins to freeze; December to March is snowy and cold.

CRIME AND SAFETY

Moscow is probably safer than most major European capitals. Take the normal precautions for any large metropolis. Change money only in marked change booths, and be sure to count the cash that you take from the sliding drawer (there is a scam in which one bank note gets stuck in the drawer thanks to a bit of glue). Do not fall for another scam in which a large wad of bills is 'dropped' on the street; if you pick it up, the person who 'dropped it' will return and insist the sum was twice what you've just picked up.

Nationalism and racism are becoming a serious problem. Skinheads with shaved heads wearing black or military-style clothing prey on black and Asian people. Avoid groups of them, particularly at night on the metro.

While terrorist attacks are a serious problem in the south of the country, there have also been incidents in Moscow. Visitors are advised to be cautious and aware in airports, the metro and other crowded public spaces.

If you are robbed, you'll need to go to the police precinct to file a report and get a spravka, an official document registering the crime (which you'll need for the insurance settlement).

I've been robbed. Меня ограбили. **Menya ograbili.**
My passport/visa was stolen. Украли мой паспорт/мою визу.
Ukrali moy passport/moyu visu.
I need a document from the militia about the crime for my
insurance Чтобы получить страховку, мне нужна справка
из полиции. **Chtoby poluchit strakhovku, mne .nuzhna
spravka iz politsii.**

D

DISABLED TRAVELLERS

Moscow is not a disabled person-friendly city. The Marriott chain, Holiday Inn, and several other hotels have comfortable wheelchair accessible rooms and public spaces; a few restaurants and museums have ramps, but the majority do not. Since tourists in wheelchairs will need to be carried upstairs, it is recommended to bring a lighter manual chair. Up-to-date information can be found at www.perspektiva-inva.ru.

DRIVING

Moscow is a difficult city for drivers: the traffic is appalling; the roads are badly maintained but seem to be constantly under construction; the drivers are reckless and aggressive. Not surprisingly, Russia's rate of fatal road accidents is about 10 times higher than Britain's.

Rules and regulations. Should you wish to take the challenge, you should have an International Licence, know that traffic drives on the right, seat belts are mandatory, and the speed limit within cities is 60kph (38mph), and up to100kph (62mph) on the outer Ring Road (MKAD) and major thoroughfares, unless otherwise marked. Left turns are usually not allowed unless marked or indicated with an arrow on the traffic light.

E

ELECTRICITY

Russia has 200V/50Hz AC, with European-style round two-pin sockets but some sockets are narrower than European standard pins; ask the reception desk for an adaptor (переходник – perekhodnik).

EMBASSIES AND CONSULATES

Australia: Podkolokolny pereulok 10A/2, tel: 495-956 6070, www.russia.embassy.gov.au.

Canada: Starokonyushenny pereulok 23, tel: 495-105 6000, www.canadainternational.gc.ca/russia-russie/index.aspx.

Ireland: Grokholsky pereulok 5, tel: 495-937 5911, www.embassyofireland.ru.

New Zealand: Ulitsa Povarskaya 44, tel: 495-956 3579, www.nzembassy.com/russia.

South Africa: Granatny pereulok 1, str. 9, tel: 495-540 1177, www.saembassy.ru.

UK: Smolenskaya naberezhnaya 10, tel: 495-956 7200, www.ukinrussia.fco.gov.uk.

US: Bolshoy Devyatinsky pereulok 8, tel: 495-728 5000, moscow.usembassy.gov.

EMERGENCIES

There are four emergency numbers that are standard for all Russia, although only the police (02) have a 24-hour English-speaking operator in Moscow.

Fire **01**
Police **02**
Ambulance **03**
Gas **04**

G

GAY AND LESBIAN TRAVELLERS

Homosexuality was a crime in Soviet times and is still condemned by the Russian Orthodox Church and many Russians. Skinheads and religious groups have targeted some gay clubs in Moscow and have attacked clients when they leave, and that the police are sometimes indifferent (or worse) to complaints from gays and lesbians. However, attitudes are changing and there is a lively gay club scene. The site www.gay.ru has an extensive English-language section with listings. For more information, contact Together at together@gay.ru.

GETTING THERE

By air. Direct daily flights from London arrive in Moscow every day via Aeroflot (www.aeroflot.ru) and British Airways (www.britishairways.com) and from New York via Aeroflot (www.aeroflot.ru). Tickets average about $400 from the UK, and about $900 from the US, but 'specials' or flying another European airline with a stopover can bring down the price considerably. There are no direct flights from Canada, Australia and New Zealand.

By rail. Trains from Baltic and East European countries take between 15 and 37 hours. Be aware that you'll need a transit visa obtained ahead of time to pass through Belarus. A train from Helsinki to Moscow via St Petersburg takes 17 hours. From the east, trains from Beijing and Vladivostok make the week-long trip several times a week.

GUIDES AND TOURS

Many companies provide package tours to Moscow that include visa, hotel, meals and tours. For individual tourists, Capital Tours provides daily English-language city tours, tours of the Kremlin and Armoury Museum as well as other excursions. Check their site for the meeting point (Gostiny Dvor, Ilinka ulitsa 4, entrance 6, tel: 495-232 2442, www.capitaltours.ru). Patriarshy Dom provides several high-quality, unique English-language tours a day, as well as day and overnight trips outside the city (tel: 495-795 0927, www.toursinrussia.com). Another option is a freelance guide. Check on the forums at www.expat.ru, or www.waytorussia.net. Guides usually charge about $15 per hour and can often provide a car and driver at extra cost.

H

HEALTH AND MEDICAL CARE

No vaccinations are compulsory for Moscow and Russia, and there are no country-specific health risks. The tap water is certified as safe, but most people filter it; inexpensive mineral water (минеральная вода – mineralnaya voda) is available almost everywhere. Pharmacies are plentiful and sell many common Western OTC drugs. The 36.6 stores are good Western-style chemists. All-night pharmacies are in every district; look for the number '24' or ask at your hotel. Be sure that you have medical insurance that covers you abroad and includes medical evacuation. Russian health care is underfinanced and patchy; in case of illness, it is strongly recommended that you seek help at a clinic catering to foreigners. Bring insurance forms with you; in most cases you will have to pay for the services and be reimbursed by your carrier upon return home.

American Medical Center, Prospect Mira 26, str.6, tel: 495-933 7700.

European Medical Centre, Spiridonsky pereulok 5, tel: 495-933 6655.

US Dental Care, Bolshaya Dmitrovka ulitsa 7/5, korpus 4 tel: 495-933 8686.

Where's the nearest (all night) pharmacy? Где ближайшая (круглосуточная) аптека? **Gde blizhayshaya (kruglosutochnaya) apteka?**
I need a doctor/dentist Мне нужен врач/зубной врач. **Mne nuzhen vrach/zubnoi vrach.**
an ambulance скорая помощь **skoraya pomoshch**
a hospital больница **bolnitsa**

L

LANGUAGE

Since Moscow is still not totally geared to foreign tourists and most signs are only in Russian, basic familiarity with the alphabet is strongly recommended.

In this guide, we have used the simplified system of transliteration provided below. Note that many male Russian names and adjectives end in -ой, –ий or –ый, which we transliterate as 'y'. In some cases, letters are transliterated as pronounced, such as the endings –oro, -ero (-evo, -ovo) and some names, like Tchaikovsky or Gorbachev, are given in the form that has become standard in English. Don't worry about soft and hard sounds; if you can hit most of the consonants in a word, people will understand you.

Russian – *Transliteration* – English Example

А а *a* a in father

Б б *b* b in book

В в *v* v in very

Г г *g* g in good

Д д *d* d in day

Е е *e* (Ye when first letter in a word) ye in yet (note that words like 'lobnoe' are pronounced lob-noi-ye)

Ё ё *yo* yo in yonder

Ж ж *zh* s in pleasure or composure

З з *z* z in zoo

И и *i* ee in meet

Й й *y* y in boy

К к *k* k in kite

Л л *l* l in lamp

М м *m* m in map

Н н *n* n in not

О о *o* o in pot

П п *p* p in pet

Р р *r* r in restaurant (rolled r)

С с *s* s in sound

Т т *t* t in tip

У у *u* oo in hoot

Ф ф *f* f in face

Х х *kh* ch in Channukah (a guttural kh)

Ц ц *ts* ts in sits

Ч ч *ch* ch in chip

Ш ш *sh* sh in shut
Щ щ *shch* shch in fresh cheese
Ъ ъ Placed after a consonant, this keeps the sound hard
Ы ы *y* i in ill
Ь ь Placed after a consonant, this makes the sound palletized (soft)
Э э *e* e in extra
Ю ю *yu* u in use
Я я *ya* ya in yard

> Hello Здравствуйте **Zdravstvuyte**
> Good morning Доброе утро **Dobroe utro**
> Good day/evening Добрый день/вечер **Dobry den/vecher**
> Good bye До свидания **Do svidaniya**
> Please Пожалуйста **Pozhaluysta**
> Thank you Спасибо **Spasibo**
> Help! Помогите! **Pomogite!**
> Good/bad Хорошо/плохо **Khorosho/plokho**
> I don't understand Я не понимаю **Ya ne ponimayu**
> Open/closed Открыто/закрыто **Otkryto/zakryto**
> Entrance/exit Вход/выход **Vkhod/vykhod**
> Cashier/ticket office Касса **Kassa**

M

MONEY

The currency is the rouble, consisting of 100 kopeks. Bills are in denominations of 10, 50, 100, 500, 1000, and 5000, and coins of one, five, 10, and 50 kopeks, as well as one, two, five and 10 roubles.

Major credit cards are generally accepted at many hotels, shops and restaurants but in some cases they aren't, so it's best to ask in advance. Only **exchange** money at official exchange offices (обмен – obmen), in banks or hotels.

I'd like to exchange money. Я хочу обменять деньги.
Ya khochu obmenyat dengi.
Do you accept credit cards? Вы принимаете кредитные
карты? **Vy prinimaete kreditnye karty?**
Can I cash traveller's cheques? Можно обналичить
дорожные чеки? **Mozhno obnalichit dorozhnye cheki?**

O

OPENING TIMES

There are no standard opening and closing times. **Banks and state offices** open from 8.30am and close at 6 or 7pm, often with an hour off for lunch. Most **shops** open around 10 or 11am and close at 8 to 10pm; a few still close for lunch. **Restaurants** usually stay open until the last client leaves, and there are hundreds of 24-hour kiosks, produce stores, cafés and clubs. Each **museum** has its own idiosyncratic hours, and is usually closed one or two days a week, plus one additional 'cleaning' day per month. Museums stop selling entry tickets an hour before closing.

P

POLICE

The local police (полиция – *politsiya*) often stop pedestrians for document checks. Hand them your documents but not your purse or wallet (money has been known to disappear during the check). Despite their uneven reputation, most Russian police try their best to be helpful if you're lost or in trouble (though few speak English). The main police headquarters are at Ulitsa Petrovka 38, tel: 495-694 9229.

PUBLIC HOLIDAYS

Russian state holidays (when banks, state offices and many stores and services are closed) are:

1–7 January New Year and Orthodox Christmas
23 February Defenders of the Homeland Day
8 March International Women's Day
1 May Spring and Labour Holiday
9 May Victory Day
12 June Russia Day
4 November People's Unity Day

When holidays fall on Tuesday or Thursday, Monday or Friday are usually days off, with the Saturday after the holiday a work day. Note that embassies are closed on both Russian and national holidays. For festivals and church holidays see page 97.

T

TELEPHONES

For local calls, public telephones can be found near and in metro stations. You can buy a phone card (телефонная карта – *telefonnaya karta*) at the ticket booth in denominations of 20 and 50 minutes. To call outside the country, dial 8 and wait for the dial tone to repeat, then 10, then the country and city codes and number. The country code for Russia is 7; Moscow has two city codes, 495 and 499.

TIME ZONES

Moscow is GMT plus three hours. In 2014 Russia ceased observing the Daylight Saving Time and switched to permanent standard time, so the time differences should be recalculated in the summer months.

New York	London	Johannesburg	**Moscow**	Sydney	Auckland
4am	9am	11am	**noon**	8pm	10pm

TIPPING

Tipping in Moscow is rather haphazard: expected but not mandatory. In restaurants and cafes, a service charge is sometimes added to the bill; otherwise 10–15 percent is ample.

TOILETS

Public toilets (usually blue plastic), for which you pay, are found by metro stations and in most public parks. Facilities in museums, restaurants, cafés, and bars are generally clean, but may not always have toilet paper in each booth. The men's room is marked by the letter M and the women's room by the letter Ж.

TOURIST INFORMATION

The Moscow Tourism and Hotel Industry Committee has a 24-hour hotline (8-800-220 0002) with English-speaking consultants and www.moscow.info, a tourism website sponsored by the city government, has information on sights, listings and travel services. There is a Volunteer Tourist Centre of the Moscow City in Kronshtadtsky **ploshchad** 43A. Area maps can be found on stands outside most metro stations. The Russian National Tourist Office has an office in London (202 Kensington Church Street, London W8 4DP, tel: 207-985 1234, www.visitrussia.org.uk). In the US, a commercial organization represents the tourist authority, the Russian National Group (224 West 30th Street, suite 701, New York, NY, 10001, tel: 877-221 7120, www.russia-travel.com).

TRANSPORT

Metro. The stations are marked with a red 'M'. Inside the station, buy a ticket at the booth for up to 20 journeys, regardless of distance (hold up fingers for the number of journeys), press the card against the round sensor on the turnstile, and hop on the fast-moving escalator. The metro runs from 5.25am to 1am. (Moskovsky Metropoliten, www.mosmetro.ru, enquiries: 495-539 5454).

Street transport. Tickets are sold for trams, trolleys and buses in

Where can I get a taxi? Где можно найти такси? **Gde mozhno nayti taksi?**
What's the fare to... ? Сколько стоит проезд до...? **Skolko stoit proezd do...?**
Where is the nearest bus stop/metro station? Где ближайшая остановка автобуса/станция метро? **Gde blizhaishaya ostanovka avtobusa/stantsiya metro?**

front of metro stations. In some buses you put the ticket in the gate at the door; in others you hand the ticket to a conductor or pay the driver (watch your fellow travellers to see what system is in place). In mini-vans (маршрутки – *marshrutki*) you pay the driver directly. Street transportation runs from about 5am to about 1.30am (depending on the specific route). (Mosgortrans: www.mosgortrans. ru, enquiries: 495-539 5454, lost and found: 499-264 8285)

Taxis, identified by the checker design and 'T' on the roof, cluster around hotels and a few main squares. It is difficult to catch a cab cruising the streets. However, if you stand on the road and hold your hand out, in a few minutes 'private cab drivers' (i.e., someone moonlighting in his own car) will undoubtedly stop. Despite the apparent danger, this is the standard way Muscovites get around the city. The only safety precaution is avoiding any car with one or more additional passengers. State your destination and your price (usually around 300 roubles for a short distance, up to 700 or more for a long distance or at night) and hop in.

V

VISA AND ENTRY REQUIREMENTS

Before you go. All visitors to Russia must have a visa, a passport valid for six months after departure and at least two free pages for the visa and stamps. If you arrange your trip through an agency, the agency will handle all the visa formalities for you. If you are arranging your own travel, you will have to book the hotel and round-trip ticket before applying for the visa. Full instructions are listed on Russian embassy sites in each country; they vary by country and have changed several times recently, so check for current rules. Tourist visas, which range in price depending on the country and turnaround time (average cost is about $100), are issued for up to one month and cannot be extended. Although visas can be processed within one day, allow several weeks. You can also use companies such as Way to Russia (www.waytorussia.net) or hotels that provide visa support and registration.

Upon arrival. When you arrive, you must to fill out a migration card. Airlines provide them onboard and help you fill them out. You must be registered during your stay. This is arranged by hotels or the inviting agency (including visa and tour companies and most apartment rental agencies). A receipt proves legal registration.

Customs. Fill out a customs declaration for any cash and traveller's cheques over $10,000. Use the Red Channel at the airport and have your declaration stamped. When you leave, you will have to fill out a form if you are taking out more than $3,000. You must not take out more money than you brought in without a stamped document from the bank (if you withdrew cash) or other certification that you received the money legally. ATM receipts are not valid proof.

You may take out of the country only 250 grams of black caviar per person in factory-sealed jars and 'a reasonable amount' of red caviar, also in factory-sealed jars. You may not take out any antiques more than 50 years old or fine art without permission of the Ministry of Culture. Permission can be arranged in the finer galleries and shops, although it takes at least five days (and usually longer). Keep receipts for any expensive souvenirs.

Documents. By the time you get to your hotel, you will have a collection of documents: visa, migration card, passport, registration receipt and possibly customs form. It's a good idea to make copies of all these documents in your hotel and leave them in the hotel safe. You should carry your passport, visa, registration receipt and migration card with you at all times; it's also a good idea to carry a card with your hotel name and address in case you get lost. If your documents are lost or stolen, you will have to go to a police precinct to get an official document of theft/loss and to your Embassy for a new passport and assistance replacing your Russian documents.

W

WEBSITES AND INTERNET ACCESS

Virtually all hotels and post offices have Internet access, and throughout the city you will find Wi-Fi signs in cafés and coffee shops.
There are many sites with information about Moscow in English:
www.moscow.info For official city tourist information.
www.gotorussia.com and www.expat.ru Both have helpful information and forums.
www.themoscowtimes.com Up-to-date news and culture.
www.accuweather.com The best weather advisory.
You can preview museums at www.russianmuseums.info, www.kreml.ru, www.tretyakovgallery.ru, www.saintbasil.ru and www.arts-museum.ru.

Y

YOUTH HOSTELS

Moscow has several good and cheap youth hostels. Try Godzillas Hostel (Bolshoy Karetny pereulok 6, 1st floor, tel: 495-699 4223, www.godzillashostel.com); Napoleon Hostel (Maly Zlatoustinsky pereulok 2, 4th floor, tel: 495-628 6695, www.napoleonhostel.com) or Hostel Moscow (Gogolevsky bulvar 33/1, 4th floor, tel: 916-188 4333, www.hostel-moscow.com). Information about hostelling in Russia can be found on the Youth Hostels Association of Russia website (www.russia-hostelling.ru).

RECOMMENDED HOTELS

Moscow's city centre hotels can be very expensive. An economic alternative is a serviced apartment, which might be a bit daunting for a first-time visitor, but can provide comfort and convenience for an affordable price (see page 116). Hotels and apartments can be booked directly on-line, through internet hotel agencies, or through tourist agencies. Prices are usually listed in roubles; sometimes they are listed in 'currency units', which the hotel itself defines. Be sure to enquire about the hotel exchange rate so you know the cost in your currency and clarify if the quoted price includes the 18 percent VAT tax.

The hotels listed provide Wi-Fi and breakfast unless otherwise noted, along with support when applying (in advance) for your visa.

As a basic guide we have used the symbols below to indicate the price per night for a double room with bath.

$$$$	over $400
$$$	$250–400
$$	$125–250
$	under $125

CITY CENTRE

Assambleya Nikitskaya $$$ *Bolshaya Nikitskaya 12, str. 2, tel: 495-933 5001*, www.assambleya-hotels.ru. This 30-room boutique hotel is located two blocks from the Kremlin in the former mansion of Prince Menshikov, Peter the Great's favourite. The interior is classical, with good-sized rooms and a cosy bar in the lobby.

Bentley Hotel $$ *Ulitsa Pokrovka 28/6 str. 3, tel: 495-917 4436*, www.bentleyhotel.ru. A beautifully restored manor house with 16 surprisingly affordable rooms within easy walking distance of the city's main sights. There is a pleasant lobby bar and, for those who miss Western food, a 24-hour American diner on the premises.

Budapest $$$ *Petrovskie linii 2/18, tel: 495-729 3501*; www.hotel-budapest.ru. Close to the city centre, this late 19th-century building offers old-world charm with individual rooms, each different, remodelled in classic décor. There is a full range of services, and an accommodating staff. A fitness centre at the sister hotel, Petr I, is available to Budapest guests.

East West $$$$ *Tverskoy bulvar 14, str. 4, tel: 495-690 0404,* www. hotel-east-west.ru. This small and charming hotel in a former classical mansion has a variety of rooms, some rather small, and no fitness centre. Its location just off Tverskaya ulitsa makes it attractive for tourists and business people.

Golden Apple $$$$ *Malaya Dmitrovka 11, tel: 495-980 7000,* www. goldenapple.ru. This super-stylish boutique hotel off Pushkin Square is furnished in 21st-century high-tech luxury, down to the bathroom fixtures. In addition to the standard amenities, the Golden Apple has a spa fitness centre, swish bar and restaurant. Breakfast not included.

Kebur Palace $$$ *Ulitsa Ostozhenka 32, tel: 495-733 9070,* www. keburpalace.ru. Formerly the Tiflis, this private boutique hotel is very pleasant. Some rooms overlook a patio filled with flowers and a fountain in the summer, and it is located in a quiet old aristocratic neighbourhood with cafés, shops and embassies. Modern rooms and a spa-standard fitness club, pool and sauna.

Kitay-Gorod $$ *Lubyansky proezd 25, tel: 495-991 9971,* www.otel-kg.ru. This 46-room hotel is nicely situated a few blocks from Red Square, very close to the metro station with plenty of shops, cafés, and restaurants. The rooms are modern and bright, with a friendly staff.

Klub 27 $$$$ *Ulitsa Malaya Nikitskaya 27, tel: 495-695 5650,* www. club27.ru. This charming boutique hotel in a restored manor house is located in a quiet aristocratic neighbourhood a short walk from the US, UK and NZ embassies.

Marco Polo Presnja $$$$ *Spiridonevsky pereulok 9, str. 1, tel: 495-660 0606,* www.presnja.ru. A hotel for British and American governesses and visitors before the Revolution, then a Party hotel, the Marco Polo has seamlessly updated Soviet décor (marble columns with cheerful colours) in this small (68-room) hotel. It has non-smoking rooms, fitness centre and sauna, and is on a quiet street near the Patriarshy ponds neighbourhood.

Marriott Courtyard $$$$ *Voznesensky pereulok 7, tel: 495-981 3300,* www.courtyardmoscow.com. A surprisingly large (218-room) hotel tucked down a small side street, just a few blocks from the Kremlin, featuring a large, pleasant, airy atrium courtyard, a good-sized fitness centre and several restaurants. Breakfast not included.

Marriott Tverskaya $$$$ *Pervaya Tverskaya Yamskaya ulitsa 34, tel: 495-258 3000.* The more modest of several Marriott hotels in the city centre, the Tverskaya has a spacious open atrium and a homely atmosphere. Breakfast not included.

Metropol $$$$ *Teatralny proezd 1, tel: 495-266 0168,* www.metropol-moscow.ru. Beautifully restored style moderne building right off Red Square. Some of the standard rooms are very small, but the location and public rooms are spectacular and filled with history.

Moscow Point – Red October $$ *Bersenevsky pereulok 3/10, str. 8, tel: 499-499 4901,* www.moscowpoints.com. This mini, second-floor hotel is in the heart of the art scene at Bolotny Island, and has eight large, sleek rooms. Each room has a view of the Moscow River and skyline, but a bit of a trek to metro stations.

Hotel National $$$$ *Mokhovaya ulitsa 15/1, str. 1, tel: 495-258 7000,* www.national.ru. The elegant style moderne hotel was home to the first Soviet leaders right after the 1917 Revolution and then a rather dreary hotel during the Soviet period where Eloise lived in Kay Thompson's Eloise in Moscow. Today it has been restored to pre-Revolutionary splendour.

Petr I $$$$ *Neglinnaya ulitsa 17, str. 1, tel: 495-925 3050,* www.hotel-peter1.ru. The sister hotel to the Budapest provides a higher standard and price, modern décor, but the same excellent location.

Sretenskaya Hotel $$$ *Ulitsa Sretenka 15, tel: 495-933 5544,* www.hotel-sretenskaya.ru. This small boutique hotel of 38 modern rooms has public spaces that evoke pre-Petrine Russia and a lush, decidedly non-Muscovite tropical atrium. The hotel has a sauna and gym, and is located in a historical district with lots of cafés and shops, about 30 minutes from Red Square on foot.

OUTSIDE THE GARDEN RING ROAD

Ampir Belorusskaya $$$ *1-aya Brestskaya ulitsa 60, str. 1, tel: 499-251 6413,* www.ampir-belorusskaya.ru. This small, 33-room hotel is on a busy street, one block away from the main street of Tverskaya and near the Belorussian train station. The dark red, blue and gold décor exudes a similar ambience to that of an English gentleman's club.

Azimut Olympic Hotel $$$$ *Olimpiysky prospekt 18/1, tel: 495-931-9000,* http://en.azimuthotels.com. The hotel has nearly 500 rooms, including non-smoking rooms, a fitness centre, a business centre and plenty of cafés, bars and restaurants. Free Wi-Fi. Although a 15-minute walk to the nearest metro station, the city centre is just a 10-minute taxi or bus journey.

Garden Ring Hotel $$$ *Prospekt mira 14, str. 2, tel: 495-988 3460,* www.gardenringhotel.ru. An elegant mid-sized hotel with an empire-style feel, the hotel has large rooms, a full-service spa and pool, and several restaurants, including a summer terrace during the good weather. Just outside the Garden Ring Road, it is close to a metro station, shops and restaurants, and a 30-minute walk to the city centre.

Holiday Inn $$$ *Lesnaya ulitsa 15, tel: 495-783 6500,* www.holiday-inn.com. Located near the city centre, the 120-storey, 200-bed hotel is rather soulless, but with a reasonable level of service and comfort, including a small fitness centre and business centre. Breakfast not included.

Novotel Novoslobodskaya $$$ *Novoslobodskaya ulitsa 23, tel: 495-780 4000,* www.novotel.com. Although slightly outside the city centre, this standard Novotel is next to a metro station in a lively neighbourhood. It has a good-sized gym and sauna and a top-floor bar with spectacular views of the city.

Sheraton Palace Hotel $$$$ *1-aya Tverskaya-Yamskaya ulitsa 19, tel: 495-931 9700,* www.sheratonpalace.ru. The Sheraton Palace was built in 1993 on the main street a block from the Belorussian train station. It provides standard international level service, including exercise facilities. It is right in the heart of the city centre.

Sovietsky $$ *Leningradsky prospekt 32/2, tel: 495-960 2000,* www.sovietsky.ru. Classic Stalinist era hotel with spacious, rather old-fashioned rooms (Soviet grand style), located not far from the city centre, but between metro stations. Added value: a full range of services and the Yar restaurant.

SOUTH OF THE RIVER

Baltschug Kempinski $$$$ *Ulitsa Balchug 1, tel: 495-287 2000,* www.kempinskimoscow.com. This large and elegant hotel is just across the Moscow River from the Kremlin with some spectacular views of St Basil's Cathedral and equally spectacular luxury. The hotel offers a spa-standard fitness centre with pool and sauna. Breakfast included with certain rates.

Grand Victoria $$ *Ulitsa Shchipok 16, tel: 499-784 5202,* www.grandvictoria.ru. In 2003 a former merchant's house was turned into this family-style hotel with a bright antique décor. The modern rooms are all 'non-standard' and vary in shape, size and price. There is a sauna, billiard room and small pool. Two blocks from Paveletsky train station and the Garden Ring Road, it is a 10-minute metro or cab ride to the city centre.

Kadashevskaya Hotel $$$ *Kadashevskaya naberezhnaya 26, tel: 499-287 0510,* www.kadashevskaya.com. The exterior of this manor house on the canal across from Red Square is traditional, but the interior is sleek, comfortable modernism. There is a fitness centre and sauna as well as a popular Italian restaurant.

Hotel Katerina City $$–$$$ *Shlyuzovaya naberezhnaya 6/1, tel: 495-795 2444,* www.hotel-katerina.ru. Located on the embankment across the river from Red Square, this mid-sized hotel has small, brightly coloured rooms, sauna and fitness centre, and a friendly staff that tries to please.

Medea Hotel $$ *Pyatnitskaya ulitsa 4, str. 1, tel: 495-232 4898,* www. medea-hotel.ru. Extremely charming, small (21-room) boutique hotel, once an old merchant's house, not far from the Tretyakov Gallery (metro stations Tretyakovskaya and Novokuznetskaya), across the river from the Kremlin, with a style moderne décor in public spaces and rooms.

Hotel Sputnik $$ *Leninsky prospekt 38, tel: 495-930 2287,* www.hotel sputnik.ru. The Sputnik was built in 1968 in the drab Brezhnev era and although the exterior is still undistinguished, in 2006 all the rooms and public spaces were renovated and tourist services added. A 10-minute walk to the metro station and another 10-minute ride to the city centre.

Swissotel Krasnye Holmy $$$$ *Kosmodamianskaya nab. 52, str. 6, tel: 495-787 9800,* www.moscow.swissotel.com. A luxurious, modern 35 floors topped with a bar and a fabulous 360-degree city panorama. It has a pool, spa and exercise room, business and tourist services. Near Paveletsky train station, and a 10-minute metro ride to the sights in the city centre.

Hotel Tatiana $$$ *Stremyanny pereulok 11, tel: 495-721 2500,* www. hotel-tatiana.ru. This modern new hotel with a soaring atrium interior is a bit off the beaten path, but comfortable, friendly and with good service for the price. Walk-in power showers, plus a gym and sauna, and live music in the lobby in the evenings.

CITY OUTSKIRTS

Alfa Hotel $$ *Izmaylovsky Shosse 71, korp. A, tel: 499-166 4602,* www. alfa-hotel.ru. Built for the 1980 Olympics, this enormous white building (one in a complex of four) is right next to the Partizanskaya metro (a 15-minute ride to the centre) and outdoor flea market. It has modernised rooms, lots of entertainment (bars, sauna, restaurants), and is affordably priced.

Altay $–$$ *Botanicheskaya ulitsa 41, tel: 495-482 5703,* www.altay-hotel.ru. A nicely remodelled, large hotel near VVTs and a few minutes from the Vladykino metro station (20 minutes to the city centre).

The remodelled rooms are European standard, and the hotel has non-stop bars and cafés, plus a jazz club. No visa support offered.

Art Hotel $$$ *3-aya Peschanaya ulitsa 2, tel: 495-725 0905,* www.art hotel.ru. Modern hotel outside the city centre, with European-style rooms and a friendly atmosphere. While a bit of a walk to the Sokol metro station (20 minutes), it is pleasant and comfortable.

Hotel Irbis $$ *Ulitsa Gostinichnaya 1, tel: 495-788 7272,* www.maxima hotels.ru. Like its sister hotel the Zarya, this 3-star hotel is far from the city centre but next to a metro station, and provides modern, if modest, rooms at a decent price, plus a sauna for relaxing after a hard day of tourism.

Kosmos $$$ *Prospekt Mira 150, tel: 495-234 1206,* www.hotelcosmos. ru. This 2,000-room hotel was built by French partners for the 1980 Olympics and recently remodelled. Opposite the All-Russian Exhibition Centre, it is in an undistinguished neighbourhood and a 15-minute metro ride to the city centre, but the rates are affordable and the services acceptable.

Hotel Zarya $ *Ulitsa Gostinchnaya 4, korpus 9, tel: 495-788 7272,* www.maximahotels.ru. Part of the Maxima Hotels chain, the 3-star Zarya is quite a distance from the centre but next to a metro line. It provides clean and modern rooms and all the amenities for a decent price.

Zolotoy Kolos $ *Yaroslavskaya ulitsa 34, tel: 495-617 6217,* www. zkolos.ru. Old-fashioned, friendly hotel tucked away on a side street 10 minutes' walk from the VDNKh metro station (and 15 minutes to the city centre). The rooms are Soviet style, and they do not provide visa support, but the prices are very affordable. Free Wi-Fi.

INDEX

 **POCKET GUIDE**

MOSCOW

Third Edition 2017

Editor: Tom Fleming
Author: Michele A. Berdy
Head of Production: Rebeka Davies
Picture Editor: Tom Smyth
Cartography Update: Carte
Update Production: AM Services
Photography Credits: Alamy 5M; Getty Images 5MC, 5M, 9R, 17, 22, 26, 30, 32, 34, 44, 47, 61, 84, 98, 100, 101; iStock 4TC, 4MC, 5MC, 8L, 8R, 9, 11, 18, 29, 35, 42, 51, 58, 59, 62, 70, 105; Marriott International 7TC; Mary Evans Picture Library 21; Nowitz Photography/Apa Publications 4TL, 6MC, 7T 37, 39, 41, 77; Richard Schofield/Apa Publications 6ML, 86, 87; Shutterstock 4ML, 5T, 5TC, 6TL, 6TL, 6ML, 7M, 7M, 12, 24, 38, 49, 52, 54, 56, 64, 67, 68, 72, 74, 79, 81, 82, 89, 91, 92, 94, 95; Superstock 102; Vladimir Govorukhin 15, 19
Cover Picture: Shutterstock

Distribution
UK, Ireland and Europe: Apa Publications (UK) Ltd; sales@insightguides.com
United States and Canada: Ingram Publisher Services, ips@ingramcontent.com
Australia and New Zealand: Woodslane; info@woodslane.com.au
Southeast Asia: Apa Publications (SN) Pte; singaporeoffice@insightguides.com
Hong Kong, Taiwan and China:
Apa Publications (HK) Ltd; hongkongoffice@insightguides.com
Worldwide: Apa Publications (UK) Ltd; sales@insightguides.com

Special Sales, Content Licensing and CoPublishing
Insight Guides can be purchased in bulk quantities at discounted prices. We can create special editions, personalised jackets and corporate imprints tailored to your needs. sales@insightguides.com; www.insightguides.biz

Contact us
Every effort has been made to provide accurate information in this publication, but changes are inevitable. The publisher cannot be responsible for any resulting loss, inconvenience or injury. We would appreciate it if readers would call our attention to any errors or outdated information. We also welcome your suggestions; please contact us at: berlitz@apaguide.co.uk
www.insightguides.com/berlitz

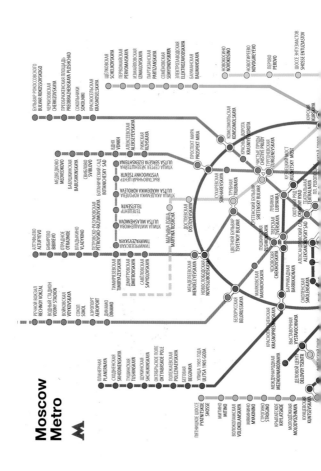

Moscow Metro

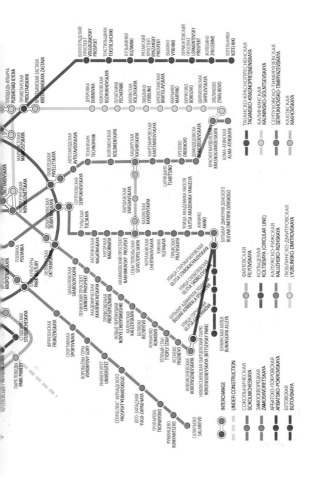

Berlitz®

speaking your language

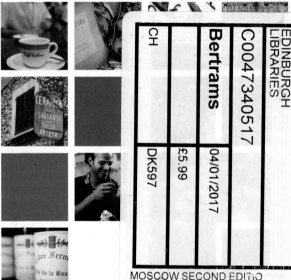

phrase book & dictionary
phrase book & CD

Available in: Arabic, Brazilian Portuguese*, Burmese*, Cantonese
Chinese, Croatian, Czech*, Danish*, Dutch, English, Filipino, Finnish*, French,
German, Greek, Hebrew*, Hindi*, Hungarian*, Indonesian, Italian, Japanese,
Korean, Latin American Spanish, Malay, Mandarin Chinese, Mexican Spanish,
Norwegian, Polish, Portuguese, Romanian*, Russian, Spanish, Swedish, Thai,
Turkish, Vietnamese
*Book only

www.berlitzpublishing.com